A Practical Guide
to Digital Design

An AVA Book

Published by AVA Publishing SA
rue du Bugnon 7
CH-1299 Crans-près-Céligny
Switzerland
Tel: +41 786 005 109
Email: enquiries@avabooks.ch

Distributed by Thames and Hudson (ex-North America)
181a High Holborn
London WC1V 7QX
United Kingdom
Tel: +44 20 7845 5000
Fax: +44 20 7845 5055
Email: sales@thameshudson.co.uk
www.thamesandhudson.com

Distributed by Sterling Publishing Co., Inc.
in USA
387 Park Avenue South
New York, NY 10016-8810
Tel: +1 212 532 7160
Fax: +1 212 213 2495
www.sterlingpub.com

in Canada
Sterling Publishing
c/o Canadian Manda Group
One Atlantic Avenue, Suite 105
Toronto, Ontario M6K 3E7

English Language Support Office
AVA Publishing (UK) Ltd.
Tel: +44 1903 204 455
Email: enquiries@avabooks.co.uk

ISBN 2-88479-039-X
10 9 8 7 6 5 4 3 2 1

Translated by Ivo Marloh, London

Production and separations by AVA Book Production Pte. Ltd., Singapore
Tel: +65 6334 8173
Fax: +65 6334 0752
Email: production@avabooks.com.sg

Acknowledgements
We thank all the artists who gave us the kind permission to reproduce their art in
this book. The design of this book was made possible with the support of
PhotoDisc, a product of Getty Images. We extend our heartfelt thanks to Thomas
Grimm, Wolfgang Neuhaus and David Neuhaus, for their patience and
understanding in recent months, characterised mainly by the work on this book.
We also thank all our students and participants of our courses, whose willingness
to experiment was inspiration for us to write this book. Furthermore we thank
Dr. Hans Faust, Dörte Fiedler and Beate Humann.

Pina Lewandowsky
Francis Zeischegg

A Practical Guide
to Digital Design

AVA Publishing SA
Switzerland

Sterling Publishing Co., Inc.
New York

CONTENTS

BASIC ELEMENTS – DOT 8

Field of vision – window of vision – passe-partout – format 11

The dot 12

Laying out several dots on the plane 13

Position, size, shape and amount of basic elements 14

From dot to plane 18

BASIC ELEMENTS – LINE 22

From dot to line 24

Text lines are lines 30

Rhythm is life 31

Overview – laying out shapes 38

Overview – effects of shapes 39

Combinatorics principle of order – permutation 40

Combinatorics principle of order – super characters 42

Combinatorics – super characters – continuous design 44

DRAWINGS, PATHS, ORIENTATION 46

Drawing, drawing, drawing... 49

Not without manual rough sketches 49

Seeing objects – drawing objects 50

Principles of animation 56

Paths, plans, orientation 58

BASIC ELEMENTS – PLANE 60

Plane division and proportions 62

Layout scribble – hand-drawn sketch 65

The format 66

Relationship between elements and the background 68

Combinatorics principle of order – variation 73

Overview – contrasts of shape 74

Overview – relationships between shapes 75

Plane and font 76

Plane and shape 82

Text as column 84

Combining elements 85

Compression 88

Analysis of motif and plane 89

Dealing with shapes 90

Rules of perception 92

BRIGHTNESS – STRUCTURE – TEXTURE 98

Brightness – tone value 100
Brightness – tone value – spatiality 102
Font and greys 104
Greys – rhythm 106
Variety of greys 108
Modulation rows 111
Spatiality – volume – perspective 114
Light and shade 116
Unusual volumes and trompe-l'oeil 117
Lines – tone values – spatiality 120
From brightness to structure 122
Systematic approach to structures and textures 124
Tactile table 126
Discovering structures 128
Analysis of motif, plane and structure 132

COLOUR 134

No colour without light 136
Colour physiology: impression and perception 138
Colour physiology: association and effect 140
Colour associations 142
The Johannes Itten colour star 148
Chromatic circle, primary, secondary and tertiary colours 149
Primary and secondary colours 151
Brightness and saturation of colour 152
Tertiary colours 154
Complementary colours – contrasting colours 156
Colour effect – colour contrasts 158
Qualitative change – colour combination and effect 165
Quantitative change – proportion and effect 166
Colour accents 168
Colour and spatiality 170
Shape and colour contrasts 172
Colour and font 174
Colour irritations 177
Transparent colours 178
Transparency and harmony 180
Harmony: chromatic-achromatic, tone-in-tone, proximity 182

MODULAR CONSTRUCTIONS 184

Modular constructions 186
Invisible nets – grid – structure 188
Geometrical shape analysis and shape development within a grid 190
Grid and guides 194
Changing shapes by masking 194
Changing shapes by dividing 195
Changing shapes by punching 195
Translation – transformation 196
(De)construction in the grid 197
Combining shape and typography 197
Combining shape and image 198
Combining shape, image and typography 198
A few words on typography 198
Tangram – playing with shapes 200
Using a grid to develop a layout 204
Setting up the baseline grid 208
Alternative grid development 209
Text formatting 210
Text alignment 210
Form, typography and layout 212

IMAGE ORGANISATION 218

Image organisation 220
Collecting and arranging 220
Placing and producing image material 220
Combining – matching – manipulating 221
Collecting by shape 222
Collecting by structure 226
Collecting by colour 232
Collecting by content or theme 236
Image contrasts 240
Perspective – position – point of view 242
Image transformation 244
Superimposing – transparency 246
Image processes 248
Image manipulation 250

BIBLIOGRAPHY, INDEX, PHOTO CREDITS 254–256

INTRODUCTION

Design work is often dismissed as something that anyone with a basic grasp of computers can do without any difficulty. Non-specialists are often asked to do design work as a result, and also on "cost" grounds. Those in charge are then often surprised when the assignment is not completed at all, or not to the standard required. This book is aimed at those who believe that acquiring a mastery of the language of visual communication – the "language of images" – requires a little more than familiarity with a few software packages. For example, people who have taught themselves or who have entered the field via an unusual route: you may have been on a few "computer courses" and learned the technique, but still feel rather in the dark when it comes to design. People who have undergone this type of "training" are easily recognised as the vast range of technical options becomes their downfall. They use software-specific solutions without really thinking and without any knowledge of the most basic principles of design.

Of course, the book is also aimed at all students of graphic design, Web design, art and film. Sooner or later, anyone working in a "creative" profession is confronted with the graphics software on the computer and has to spend some time learning how to use the programs, irrespective of what their current assignment may be: a design commission, a presentation or a film trailer. Basic design courses often fail to bridge the gap between teaching traditional techniques and computer-based techniques, and it is usually the latter that is neglected. Designers who have received thorough training can use computers to speed up the working process when carrying out conventional visual design work or pure drawing tasks. But if they experiment further they will also be able to make better use of the computer's inherent potential and perhaps develop specific forms of expression.

So, we have devised and produced this book for anyone who wants to learn and put into practice the principles of visual design with the help of the computer, whether for professional or private purposes. Our book does not concentrate on the theoretical background to visual communication; readers who are interested in this aspect will find references to some books dealing with it in the bibliography.

What are these principles of design? The purpose of the design process is to transmit visual information. It comprises analysis of the task: thinking about the content and how best to convert it into an appropriate, objective and aesthetically pleasing visual form. Solving the design problem involves choosing the right medium (to carry the information), the right design elements and arranging them. These design elements are parts of the 'language of images' that we use when creating a draft, in contrast to the language of verbal speech. The purpose of our book is to teach readers to handle these basic elements of graphic design with confidence, train perception, develop a feeling for proportion and tensions, effects and subtle differences. You will discover visual language and gain the ability to communicate deliberately and effectively.

Tip: Always print the results of your work. Make yourself a folder with dividing sheets so that you have one section for each chapter of this book. Store the results of your work in the appropriate section.

The material contained in this book is focused purely on learning the regularities of perception and the principles of design, acquiring practical experience with basic visual shapes, aspects and graphic codes. Without this knowledge and a feel for composition you will be unable to produce professionally convincing designs or achieve the desired effect, however competent you may be in using software. Learning this language of images is therefore one of the essential conditions for successful design.

When drafting and scribbling you should continue to use conventional materials like paper, pencil, brush, scissors and glue. Our book concentrates on using computers with standard DTP applications as a tool. Computers are ideal aids to the design process, but their use is not an end in itself. You should learn the technical features of your computer so that you can use them in the most appropriate way. You will work through models that show you how to combine design work with the technical support offered by the computer. Exercises can be carried out in a number of software packages (QuarkXPress 4.1, Macromedia Freehand 10 and Adobe Photoshop 6) to help you understand the individual problems, practise solving them and to experiment. Some are illustrated as Apple Macintosh screenshots and can be carried out in the same way on the PC Windows versions of the same software. You do need to know how to perform some basic tasks before working through an exercise: creating and saving documents, setting up image and text frames, and selecting, grouping, copying, cutting, pasting, deleting and moving objects. If you do not have any experience of the software, read one of the training books recommended in the bibliography. All the exercises can also be carried out in older versions of the software or in similar programs (Adobe InDesign, Pagemaker, Illustrator, CorelDraw, CorelPhotoPaint etc.).

We hope that our compendium of principles will give you a free field to experiment in. "Free" in the sense of "free from clichés" so familiar from print- and time-based media. Novices in design and artwork are often misled by the flood of images and stream of new "tools" appearing all the time on the software market. We try to provide aesthetic pointers and stimulate new ideas by showing some examples of how contemporary artists have made comprehensive use of the basic elements, resources and principles of design. Each chapter starts with works of art – drawings, paintings, photographs – from various schools, going back as far as the Bauhaus movement and the Russian constructivists of the early 20th century, moving through the de Stijl group, the Ulm College of Design in the fifties, taking in conceptual art and minimalism and coming right up to date with the post-modern movement. These artists have their own positions in the spectrum of the design mainstream that do not lend themselves to easy imitation but draw on a fundamental and highly individual process of experience with the object in question. We hope that this approach will encourage you to approach visual phenomena with an intense focus and wish you joy in your experiments, which are a vital part of your learning experience.

1

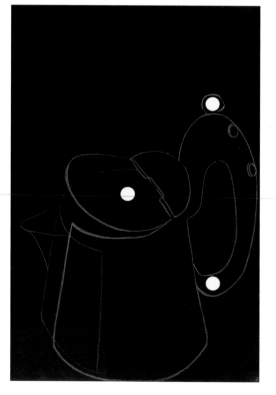

2

1/2 Nanne Meyer, from the series "Two To
Three", 1990, blackboard varnish and
colour pencil on black folio card, each
31.3 x 22 cm.
Nanne Meyer's perforated cards use holes
against a light background to compose
drawings that are organised not unlike
maps using the white "dots" as invisible
coordinates. (Printed by kind permission
of the artist.)

8

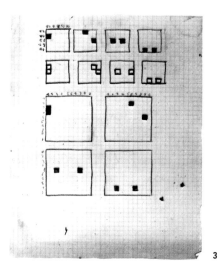

3

3 François Morellet, "Study", 1958, Pencil on checked paper, 27 x 20.9 cm.
4 François Morellet, "4 Random Distributions Of 2 Squares, Following The Numbers: 31–41–59–26–53–58–97–93", 1958, 4 plates, each 60 x 60 cm.
In François Morellet's series of drawing experiments the changing positioning of little squares in a consistent space is used to create tension. This subject matter is explored in-depth in the following chapter. (Printed by kind permission of the artist.)

4

DOTS ON A WHITE BACKGROUND – PERSPECTIVES AND PERCEPTIONS

I can objectively try to describe what I see. At the same time, what I see triggers a feeling that, irrespective of the objective facts, is simply there. Normally, we see complexly, the field of vision is not exactly outlined so that the abundance of perceived factors triggers relatively uncontrollable feelings. They can only be analysed with difficulty.

However, if we begin to break down the phenomena into detailed visual aspects in order to see their effect, we are then also able to notice and specify more clearly the perceptions and impressions that a simple visual form on a single-coloured

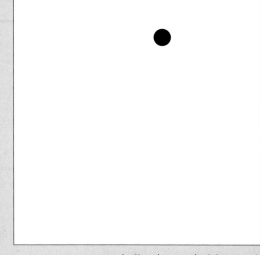

background, thus a limited plane, triggers in us. Is something hard, cool, warm, soft, coarse, calm, hectic or welcoming, repelling, intensive or boring or rough? Out the window I see snow flurries. Initially, it appears cold and cheerless. The white, untrodden wall of snow which is piling up in front of the window also has something soft, smooth and velvety about it however. Design means listening to your perceptions, abandoning preconceptions and so-called clichés and getting involved in the visual experience. In classes, students are often horrified at the first 'simple' steps. What is a format, how does it work? Shall I do it in landscape or portrait? A solitary point on a quadratic plane: what impression does the position of the point within this plane give, what feeling does it trigger? If you get involved and carry out the following experiment with other experimenters, you will find that there are phenomena which most people perceive in a similar or identical way (also see the section "Rules of Perception" on page 92).

EXERCISE **1** By turning the book, you can look at the "heavy" point in the square above in different positions within the square. Examine what feeling and impression each position triggers in you. Assign one or more of the following terms to each position of the point in the square: light, heavy, floating, oppressive, sad, happy, mobile, static, restless, calm, near, far. In what direction is the movement of the point? Away from the field or towards it? Ask acquaintances or friends their opinion. Compare with the overview "Position, size, shape and amount of basic elements" on page 14.

BASIC ELEMENTS – DOT

10

FIELD OF VISION – WINDOW OF VISION – PASSE-PARTOUT – FORMAT

To make a selection from the complete field of vision is not easy. A great help can be a movable passe-partout that you can manufacture yourself. With two angles of black card that you can move together to create a window in either portrait or landscape format or even a square, you can limit your field of vision. Colour panels in particular can be viewed and judged separately from surrounding colours with a passe-partout. Similarly you can create a passe-partout in the program Photoshop (two black angles each on a separate layer) in order to steer the attention to a specific detail. Experience has taught that these kind of devices cannot be underestimated, as the separate viewing of individual visual contexts is a core element in design.

At the same time these angles can be used to experiment with different formats and the exploration of their impacts (please also see page 62).

THE DOT

Generally we define the dot as the smallest graphical unit as well as the smallest plane unit in order to describe it visually. Kandinsky stated that a dot is born the moment the drawing tool (pen, pencil, feather) touches the paper. But the dot on its own is imaginary and not divisible, without dimension, space and form. In Dot and Line on the Surface, Kandinsky says that the dot signifies zero and embodies silence, without any element of time. A definite relationship, even tension that can stir emotion, only develops when the dot is in a format or context as you have seen in the exercise on page 10. Positioned in the centre of a format with equidistance to all edges, a dot is full of tension and emanates tranquillity. Tension and dynamics will become stronger, the more the dot is moved towards the edge: For instance, the dot can "drop out" or "fly in". Groups and formations with differing effects develop with the arrival of more dots (see exercise opposite). If the size of the dot increases in relation to the format, it becomes a plane or surface and can progress to become so dominant that it breaks the format. At the same time, the impression of background/foreground switches.

Max Bill, "Fifteen variations on one theme – variation 3", 1936–38, lithography, 30.5 x 32 cm. (Printed with kind permission of Dr. Jakob Bill. © ProLitteris, 2002, 8033 Zürich.)

LAYING OUT SEVERAL DOTS ON THE PLANE

Laying out several dots on a plane can graphically communicate different contexts. Whether a dot formation is perceived as a hierarchy or a grouping is solely a matter of arrangement. The position of each individual dot can end up ordered or disordered, symmetrical or asymmetrical.

Position

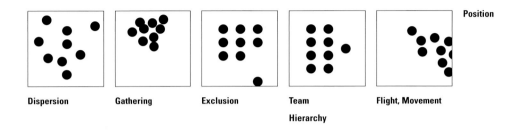

Dispersion	Gathering	Exclusion	Team	Flight, Movement
			Hierarchy	

Create 5 basic squares in an A4 document in Freehand and position 9 black dots in each of them. Assign an expression to each arrangement. With ordered arrangements you can use the command "Window → Panels → Align". Try and find different arrangements for the above mentioned expressions. You could also find other expressions and suitable arrangements.

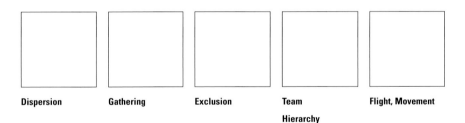

Dispersion	Gathering	Exclusion	Team	Flight, Movement
			Hierarchy	

Pay attention to the effect of symmetry and asymmetry and to the direction of motion. The easiest way to examine the effect is to enlarge the result (group each arrangement and use "Window → Panels → Transform" to enlarge each to A4-size). Stick the print-out on the wall and examine the effect.

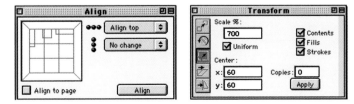

BASIC ELEMENTS – DOT

POSITION, SIZE, SHAPE AND AMOUNT OF BASIC ELEMENTS

As soon as an individual design element – regardless of whether representational or abstract – is positioned on the basic plane, a relationship develops between element and plane. Additionally, the size ratio between element and plane has different effects. If more elements are added, they in turn start to develop relationships between each other and thus spark tension and dynamism. Even force fields with attracting and opposing forces can develop if elements of varying sizes are used, depending on size and distance. Using a combination of differing sizes and number of elements can also create vibrancy. In summary, position, size, shape and amount of the design elements create effects that we can instinctively circumscribe with definite attributes. With exclusively visual elements it is therefore possible to prompt certain emotions in the viewer and communicate content.

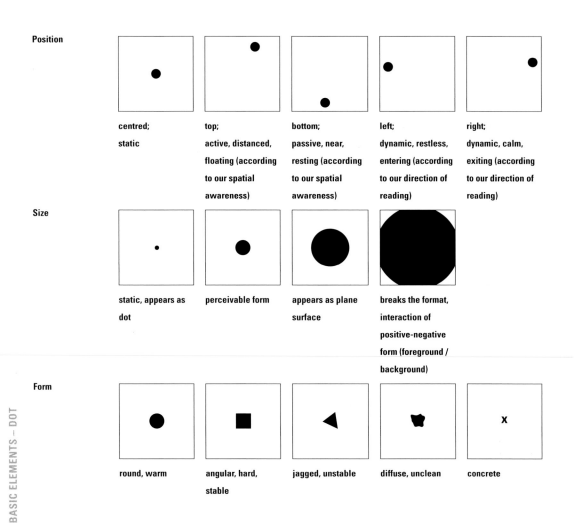

Position

centred; static

top; active, distanced, floating (according to our spatial awareness)

bottom; passive, near, resting (according to our spatial awareness)

left; dynamic, restless, entering (according to our direction of reading)

right; dynamic, calm, exiting (according to our direction of reading)

Size

static, appears as dot

perceivable form

appears as plane surface

breaks the format, interaction of positive-negative form (foreground / background)

Form

round, warm

angular, hard, stable

jagged, unstable

diffuse, unclean

concrete

If two differently sized dots are too far away, no connection is created.

Tension is created if two differently sized dots are close to each other. The attributes are emphasised – the small dot seems smaller, the large dot larger.

A calm relationship is created if the size difference between the two dots is not too large.

The two dots lose their independence and almost merge to one shape if the size difference between them is not too great and they are close together.

Size and mass

A mass of small dots can appear equal to a large dot.

Equal numbers but differing size creates more tension.

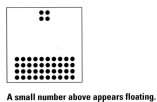

A small number above appears floating.

A large number above appears oppressive.

In two adjacent squares visualise respectively the attributes light and heavy, rich and poor, near and far. To achieve this, arrange two differently sized types of dots on a square in Freehand. Create vibrant relationships. Also work with varying amounts. **1** Open a new A4 document. Adjust the grid to 5 mm ("View → Grid → Show/Snap To Grid/Edit"). **2** Open a square of 80 x 80 mm; you can control the desired size and position in the "object-palette". Make sure to press Return (⏎) or Enter (⏎) after you have entered any changes. Give the square a black frame in the colour panel. Duplicate it by 5 (⌘⌐ D) and position the squares as shown. **3** Now open two circles, make their size 5 x 5 mm and 10 x 10 mm and give them a black fill colour in the colour panel. **4** "Copy" (⌘C) and "paste" (⌘V) the circles and arrange in the desired positions. Now print the result.

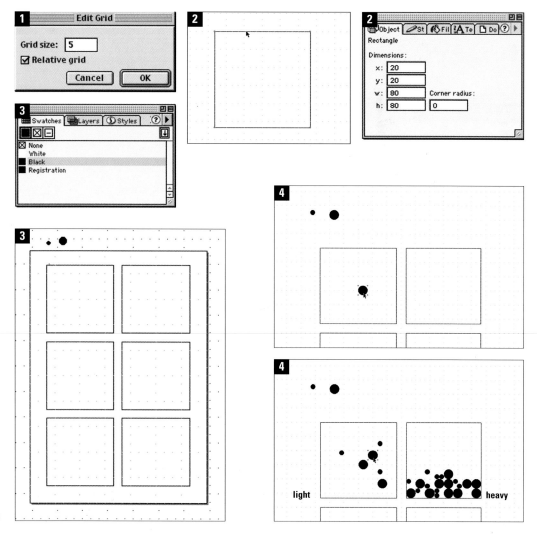

Visualise the four seasons by using different sized dots. To begin, think of typical attributes and emotions and how to describe them visually. For instance spring: everything sprouts and grows – in a vertical movement; tenderness – a lot of small dots; abundant growth – dynamically increasing dot sizes reaching beyond the scope of the format. Or winter: bright – a lot of empty space; cold – a lot of white; tranquillity – low centre of gravity, emphasis on the horizontal movement; floating snowflakes, soft – relatively evenly spaced, little tension.

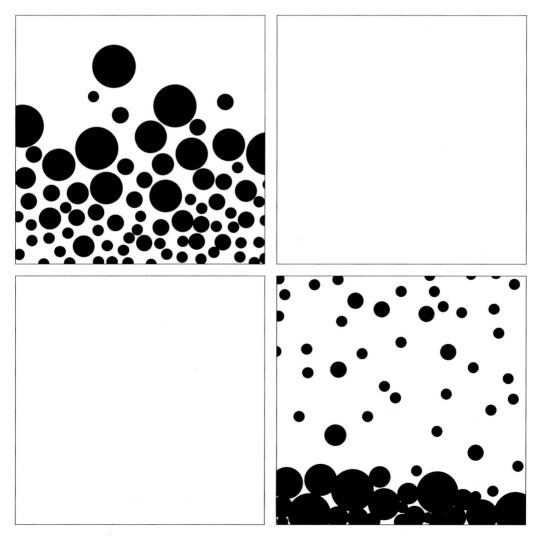

FROM DOT TO PLANE

Strictly speaking, a dot is also a surface or plane. We perceive it as a dot as long as it is relatively small and of no definable shape. The definition of its size is dependant on the relationship with and the proportion of the surrounding design elements. Used as a period in text, a dot appears even at bigger type sizes always as a dot and not as a plane. But with the increase of the dot size it can break the frame of the format and even become the background plane.

EXERCISE Create an "animation" from dot to plane by adding progressively larger dots (circular black planes) in six individual compositions. You can crop into the edge of the picture. **1** Open a new A4 document. By duplication create 6 basic squares of 80 x 80 mm as described on page 16 in point 1 and 2. Open an additional picture frame at A4 size (210 x 297 mm), make it white and send it to the back by using the command "Modify → Arrange → Send To Back". Now "Select all" (⌘A). "Join" all individual elements with the command "Modify → Join" (⌘J) to make them a single "punched" shape. **2** Open a black circle at 10 x 10 mm and position it in the square at the top left. Duplicate the circle and move it into the same position in the next square (top right). Once again duplicate the circle, enlarge it in the "Object-panel" by 5 mm (i.e. enlarge to 15 x 15 mm). Move the new circle and position vibrantly within the second square. Create more circles and increase their size by 5 mm each time. Before you go on to the next square, copy the last circle and paste into the new square – select the individual elements, copy (⌘C), and paste (⌘V). **3** If you want to crop an element, move it to

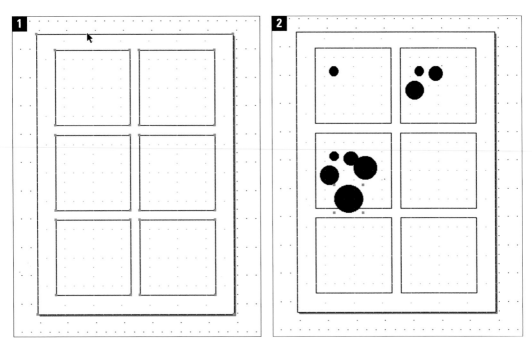

the desired position, then send it to the back by using the command "Modify → Arrange → Send To Back". **4** Continue until you have filled the last square.

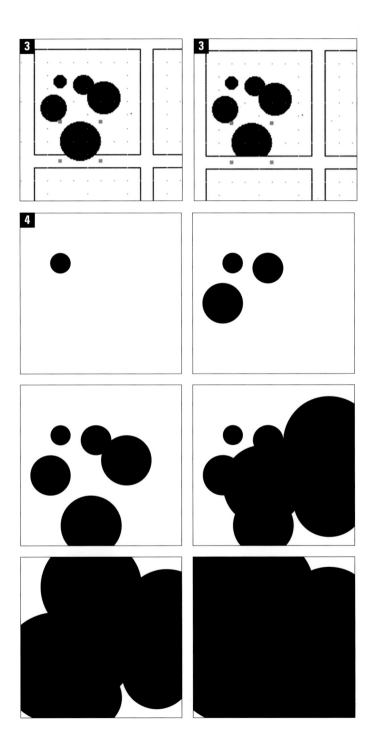

Interaction of the positive-negative form. The following exercise shows you how to use a mask to crop into a group of dots in order to find interesting and vibrant compositions. Even though the exercise is presented in Photoshop it is possible to complete it in Freehand, following the principle described on page 18. **1** Open a new A4 document (210 x 297 mm) with the resolution set to 72 dpi (dots/inch), "Mode: Greyscale", "Contents: White". Switch on the grid ("View → Show Grid"). In the preferences ("File → preferences → Guides & Grid...") set the grid to 1 cm ("Grid line every: 1 cm" and "Subdivision: 1"). Now choose the "Elliptical Marquee Tool" (⬭) and use "Add New Layer Mask". Set the foreground colour to black and open a circle, which creates a "mask". **2** Open more circles and vary the sizes. Duplicate them using the "Path-Components-Chooser-Tool" (▶) while keeping the Alt (⎚) key pressed. Position the circles vibrantly on the background until it is almost filled – but do leave a few white spaces.

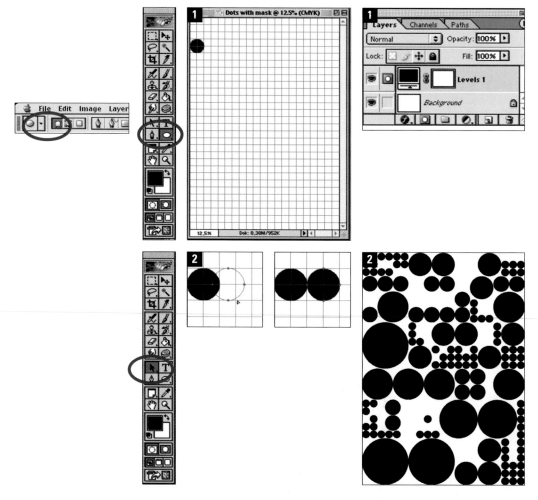

3 Open a square at 80 x 80 mm with the "Rectangular Marquee Tool", keeping the Shift key (⇧) pressed. Now click on the mask symbol in the layer panel. This creates a mask that hides everything outside of the selection. **4** Unlock the chain by clicking on the chain symbol in the layer panel but make sure to have selected the mask layer and not the form layer. Now choose 6 different and interesting parts of the overall composition by moving the mask around with the "Move Tool" (↖). Print off each one of them.

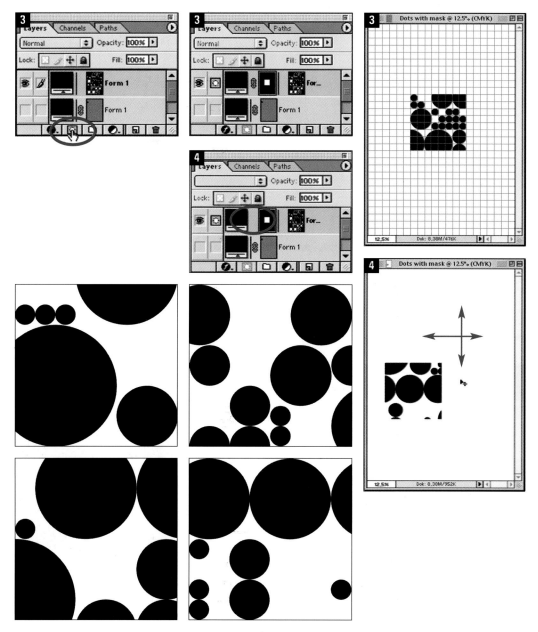

1

1 François Morellet, "Study", 1951,
gouache on paper, 2.3 x 37 cm.
2 François Morellet, "Composition", 1951,
pencil on paper, 26.8 x 37 cm.
3 François Morellet, "20 Random Lines", 1970,
oil on canvas, 240 x 240 cm.
4 François Morellet, "5 Random Lines", 1971,
oil on canvas, 140 x 140 cm.
5 A detail of François Morellet's "Study",
1959, pencil on paper, 21 x 13.4 cm.
These fragile drawings by François Morellet,
in which he explores position, texture and
properties of line, seem like microscopical
photographs. His body of work shows the
diversity and power of lines. (Printed by kind
permission of the artist.)

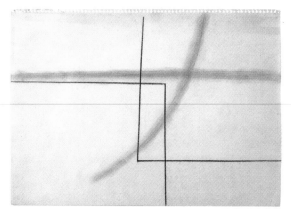

2

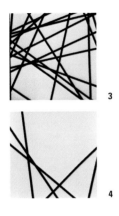

3

4

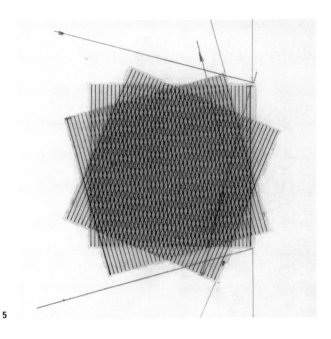

5

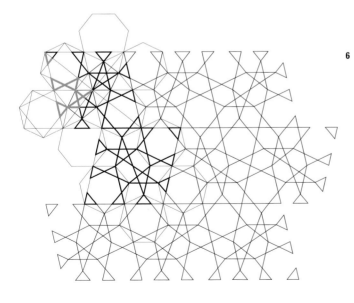

6

6 Folke Hanfeld, "7.5", 2000, vector graphic.
After looking at Folke Hanfeld's combinations of patterns for some time, they reveal a variety of geometrical relations. Unlike the exercises for combination theory and permutation in the following chapter, his statements hint at something beyond the pattern, for instance at architectural contexts. (Printed by kind permission of the artist.)

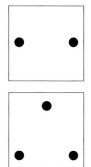

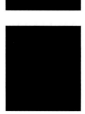

FROM DOT TO LINE

When dots are placed together with uniform spacing we do not notice every individual dot but, using imaginary lines, join them up to make a structure, a shape. Two dots, arranged on the horizontal, not too far apart, provide the simplest example of this phenomenon. In accordance with our habitual reading direction our eyes "scan" the representation – the eye movement induces us to manufacture a horizontal connection which appears to us as a line between the dots. The same phenomenon causes us to see a triangle – or even a plane – when three evenly spaced dots are arranged together. But let us stay with lines for the moment. A line is thus a structure that, unlike a dot, extends to the first dimension. In this respect the line differs from the dot for, besides size, shape, position, amount and number, it provides us with an additional design element: length. Consequently, as we will see, the vibrant compositions that we have learned are possible with dots, can be converted even more effectively and comprehensively with lines. Through repetitions and variations in spacing, length and thickness, lines lend themselves superbly to the design of rhythmic effects. The many forms of lines are classified into straight and curved lines. Text lines – straight lines of a certain thickness and brightness – can, depending on their character, also be classified as lines. The character of the line can be emphasised, or if preferred a two-dimensional effect obtained, through varying the line spacing. Make sure however that a line, similarly to the dot, keeps its proportion to the format when changing to the plane (that is becoming two-dimensional). We are going to show some examples here of straight lines and text lines in various visual exercises.

In the program Photoshop a continuous line will be produced from partially overlaid round dots. In the "Tools-Option-Palette" of painting tools, e.g. paintbrush, the painting spacing i.e. the dot spacing can be varied: 25% produces an unbroken line (standard setting); 100% puts dots next to each other without spacing.

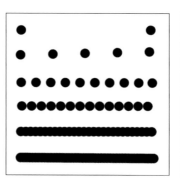

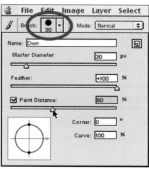

lying, passive

standing, active

dynamic, moves out (in line with our direction of reading)

powerful, aims upwards

dynamic, comes in (against our direction of reading)

powerful, falls down

bearing upwards, positive heading (in line with our direction of reading)

falling, negative heading (in line with our direction of reading)

bearing upwards, positive heading, but unusual (against our direction of reading)

falling, negative heading, but unusual (against our direction of reading)

Equally distanced parallel lines affect a gaze transverse to the direction of the lines: horizontal lines seem taller, vertical lines seem wider

Equal lines seem unequal with different positions: the vertical line seems thinnest, the horizontal line seems thickest

Lines of unequal length but equal thickness seem unequal: the longer the line, the thinner it seems in comparison

horizontal, vertical, diagonal

angular

angular, geometrically jagged

angular, jagged

thinning and thickening

Form – straight lines

curved

undulating

free

Form – curved lines

In QuarkXPress on an A4 page, create three formations, each with seven lines. **1** Begin with a black filled rectangular picture frame, 0.5 x 210 mm in size (enter the values in the "measurement palette"; a rectangle can be positioned numerically more easily than a line). The individual line thickness in the first formation should increase by 0.5 mm whilst the spaces remain uniform. Now use the command "Item → Step and Repeat..." with a vertical offset of 5 mm, each time adding the height of the rectangle, i.e. 5.5 mm. Now adjust the height of the transferred duplicate by 1 mm. Select "Step and Repeat..." again – this time with a vertical offset of 6 mm (5+1). Continue like this. **2** In the second formation the thickness of the lines as well as the spacing should be increased. Select all the objects produced in step 1 (⌘A, on active item tool). Duplicate all the objects with the command "Item → Step and Repeat..." by about 80 mm. Then select the first and second object from the new formation and use the command "Item → Space/Align...". Click the checkbox – "Vertical", select "Between: Items" and enter 5 mm under "Space". Then select the second and third object, again use the command "Space/Align..." with the same settings except for the spacing which you now need to increase by 2 or 3 mm (7 mm). Alter the spacing as follows the same way (9, 11, 13 and 15 mm). **3** In the third formation the spacing is to remain the same and the line thicknesses "progressively" grow, i.e. a line will always be twice as thick as the previous one. Duplicate the entire first formation again as in step 2, but with a vertical offset of 180 mm. Distribute the objects roughly, with sufficient distance from each other, down to the bottom format edge (the exact spacing will be determined at the end). Select the third object of the third formation and enter 2 mm under "H" (height) in the measure palette. Select the fourth object and double the height etc. again. Now select all objects in the third formation and repeat the command "Space/Align..." but with the setting "Distribute evenly" and "Between: Items". Experiment with different line thicknesses and spacing (Exercise from Paul Klee's presentations at the Bauhaus).

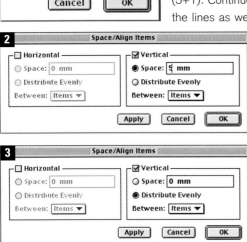

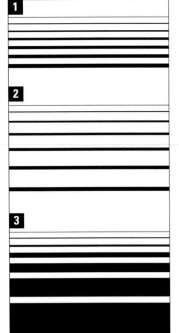

Dots can help in the creation of a line composition full of tension.
1 Open your exercise document from page 13. Draw lines through each formation that cross at least two dots and extend out of the square. **2** Delete the dots subsequently. **3** Highlight only the lines (not the square) and use the command "Edit → Cut" (⌘X). Click on the square and use the command "Edit → Paste Inside".

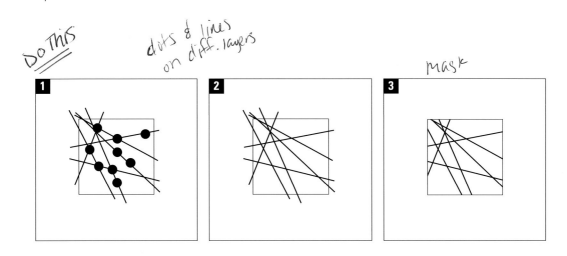

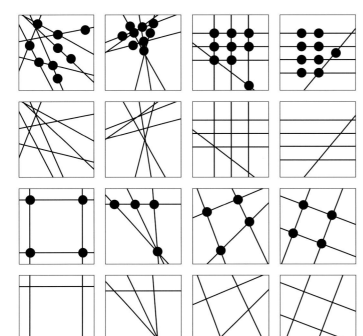

Dots and lines in ordered and unordered presentation after templates by Joost Schmidt's "Unterricht am Bauhaus" (Lessons at the Bauhaus).

Produce nine different compositions with four lines of equal length and thickness on a square base. In the next step produce nine different compositions with seven lines of equal length and thickness. First of all you can copy the compositions reproduced here. But then experiment and try to find different ones.

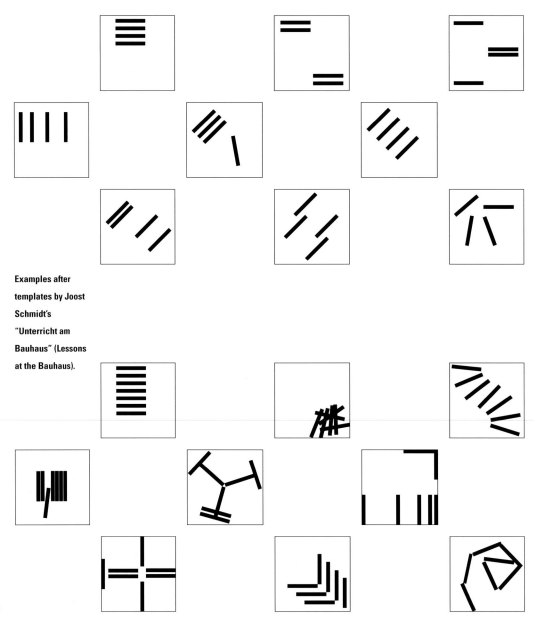

Examples after templates by Joost Schmidt's "Unterricht am Bauhaus" (Lessons at the Bauhaus).

A character is to be put together with four or more curved or straight lines of equal length. Characters of differing appearance can be developed either by gradually changing the position or rotating the lines. A further objective would be to visualise a simple sequence of movement.

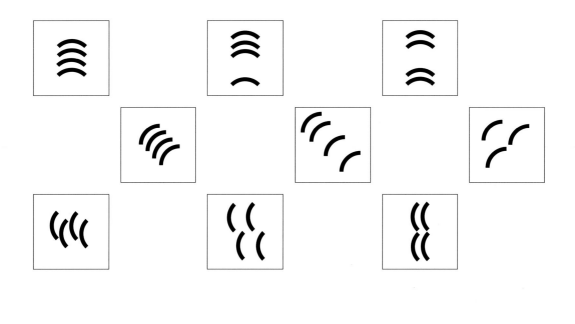

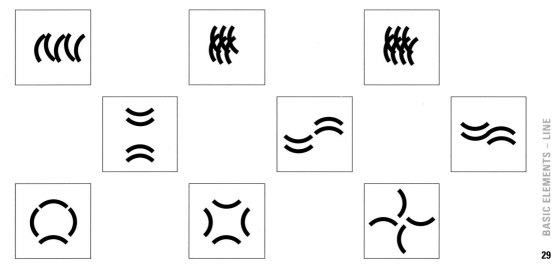

TEXT LINES ARE LINES

In character, single words, sentences and text lines are lines. In fact quite attractive lines, that do not have a monotonous or tiring effect but stimulate the eye, originate from the rhythmic repetition of individual letters and alternation of ascenders and descenders. The greater the line spacing or the reading distance to the text line, the clearer the line character becomes. If the line distance is narrower, then the individual text lines can also merge into a block, i.e. a plane. Thus composition exercises, and also designs, can be executed with lines of a particular thickness, length and greyscale instead of with text lines. Conversely powerful, expressive compositions can be created through playing around with text lines as they conform to the same natural laws of perception as lines (see page 92).

Type Size 5 pt,

Leading 5 pt = 100 % (compressed)

Si meliora dies, ut vina, poemata reddit, scire velim, chartis pretium quotus arroget annus. scriptor abhinc annos centum qui decidit, inter perfectos veteresque referri debet an inter vilis atque novos? Excludat iurgia finis, "Est vetus atque probus, centum qui perficit annos." Quid, qui deperiit minor uno mense vel anno, inter quos referendus erit? Veteresne poetas, an quos et praesens et postera respuat aetas? "Iste quidem veteres inter ponetur honeste, qui vel mense brevi vel toto est iunior anno." Utor permisso, caudaeque pilos ut equinae paulatim vello unum, demo etiam unum, dum cadat elusus ratione ruentis acervi, qui redit in fastos et virtutem aestimat annis miraturque nihil nisi quod Libitina sacravit. Ennius et sapines et fortis et alter Homerus, ut critici dicunt, leviter curare videtur, quo promissa cadant et somnia Pythagorea. Naevius in manibus non est et mentibus haeret paene recens? Adeo sanctum est vetus omne poema. ambigitur quoties, uter utro sit prior, aufert Pacuvius docti famam senis Accius alti, dicitur Afrani toga convenisse Menandro, Plautus ad exemplar Siculi properare Epicharmi, vincere Caecilius gravitate, Terentius arte. Hos ediscit et hos arto stipata theatro spectat Roma potens; habet hos numeratque poetas ad nostrum tempus Livi scriptoris ab aevo. Interdum volgus rectum videt, est ubi peccat. Si veteres ita miratur laudatque poetas, ut nihil anteferat, nihil illis comparet, errat. Si quaedam nimis antique, si pleraque

Type Size 5 pt,

Leading 7 pt = 140 %

Si meliora dies, ut vina, poemata reddit, scire velim, chartis pretium quotus arroget annus. scriptor abhinc annos centum qui decidit, inter perfectos veteresque referri debet an inter vilis atque novos? Excludat iurgia finis, "Est vetus atque probus, centum qui perficit annos." Quid, qui deperiit minor uno mense vel anno, inter quos referendus erit? Veteresne poetas, an quos et praesens et postera respuat aetas? "Iste quidem veteres inter ponetur honeste, qui vel mense brevi vel toto est iunior anno." Utor permisso, caudaeque pilos ut equinae paulatim vello unum, demo etiam unum, dum cadat elusus ratione ruentis acervi, qui redit in fastos et virtutem aestimat annis miraturque nihil nisi quod Libitina sacravit. Ennius et sapines et fortis et alter Homerus, ut critici dicunt, leviter curare videtur, quo promissa cadant et somnia Pythagorea. Naevius in manibus non est et mentibus haeret paene recens? Adeo sanctum est vetus omne poema. ambigitur quoties, uter utro sit prior, aufert Pacuvius docti famam senis Accius alti, dicitur Afrani toga convenisse

Type Size 5 pt,

Leading about 40 pt

Si meliora dies, ut vina, poemata reddit, scire velim, chartis

pretium quotus arroget annus. scriptor abhinc annos

centum qui decidit, inter perfectos veteresque referri debet

an inter vilis atque novos? Excludat iurgia finis, "Est vetus

RHYTHM IS LIFE

Rhythm is a completely fundamental means of expression: many living and natural processes are based on rhythm – we only have to think of the seasons or circadian rhythms (our heartbeat or breathing). Rhythm also plays a part when identical or similar design elements are being configured. Rhythm is found in the repetition of slightly varying design elements. The variation can be in size, shape, position or spacing for example. A rhythmic configuration is thus an emotional and vital ordering. However rhythm alone does not convey any deeper statement. For this other design methods are required, for example powerful proportion or contrasting elements.

We find very vivid rhythms for example in text lines. Rhythm lies in the word length and letter spacing. If we regard text lines of different length or the remaining empty space in the ragged setting as lines, then rhythm is be discerned here too.

Si meliora dies, ut vina, poemata reddit, scire velim, chartis pretium quotus arroget annus. scriptor abhinc annos centum qui decidit, inter perfectos veteresque referri debet an inter vilis atque novos? Excludat iurgia finis, "Est vetus atque probus, centum qui perficit annos." Quid, qui deperiit minor uno mense vel anno, inter quos referendus erit? Veteresne poetas, an quos et praesens et postera res-

My spirit soares upwards,
But love pulls it
Down again;
Sorrow bends it violently;
Thus I travel along life's arch
and then return,
to whence I came.
Friedrich Hölderlin

Text without round letters or text with letters without ascenders and descenders – the rhythm is in both cases affected.

Miliri willi wkrxyl klixi tvintrit Wikli fklimrti ritkit rirt rikftr it vitkvyit itr wliktvfirft vtrfrkri titr vilitv Exit irifii Et vittrtkvxi Fliril xywzi Yifill Eikilrivi lyxrkw vitkvyit kiliriv riwirxlik xvikliy wlixyzvill wirwr kirylix likrizi wizikriliy kirk wirk Exit fklimrti tvintrit Wittrtkyxl

nus esanes eors eaer omerus u crccun evercurare veuruo romssa caan esomna aorea aevusn manus non es menus aere aene recens eo sancum es veus omne oema amur uoens uer uro sror aueracuvus ocamam sens ccus acur ranoa convenssenano

Disturbances of the rhythm, for instance strongly varying spaces between letters (kerning) or between words as well as stair-like line endings are considered displeasing.

Si meliora dies, ut vina, poemata reddit, scire velim, chartis pretium quotus arroget annus. scriptor abhinc annos centum qui decidit, inter perfectos veteresque referri debet an inter vilis atque novos? Excludat iurgia finis, «Est vetus atque probus, centum qui perficit annos.» Quid, qui deperiit minor uno mense vel anno, inter quos referendus erit? Veteresne poetas, an quos et praesens et postera respuat aetas?

Whence I came
pulls down again;
Arch and return to
But love pulled me
Friedrich Hölderlin? No!
High above soared my spirit,
And thus I travelled along life's
And sorrow bends it violently;

On a square base design compositions with several identical or different text lines in the same font size. Then try to find terms for the sensations that the individual configurations evoke, e.g. distant, uplifting, flowing (see overview on the effect of shapes page 39).

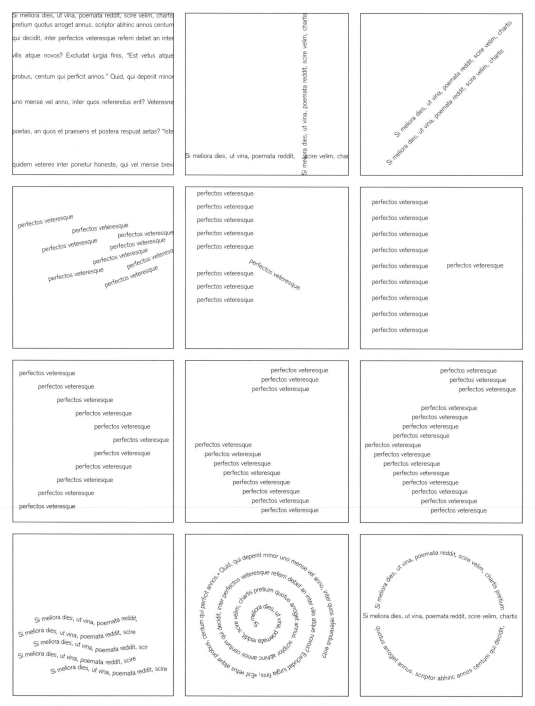

Set tabs in QuarkXPress: **1** Write a short text line in a sufficiently big text frame and put a line break at the end (⏎). Copy the line and enter it several times. **2** Leave the text frame marked and select everything (⌘A) using the active content tool (✍). Then select the command "Style → Tabs…". As well as the tab bar above the text, a dialog box will appear on top of the text box.

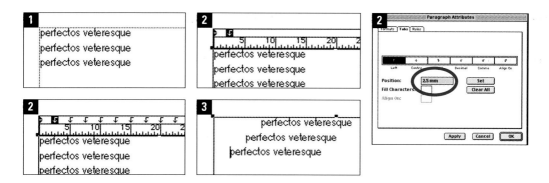

Click the tab bar to set the left justified tabs with exactly the same spacing. The tabs can be set precisely by shifting them or by entering a value in the "Position" cell. Clicking on a tab activates it; clicking on it and dragging it erases it from the tab bar. Click "OK" to leave the dialog cell. **3** Set the cursor at the beginning of the first text line and press the tab button (→|). Press it until the text line is in the required position. Repeat this with the other lines. To delete tab signs set the cursor in the required place and press the Delete or Remove button (⌫).

In Freehand justify the text in lines: **1** First draw a wavy line with the drawing pen. For further wavy lines duplicate these and modify them slightly. Write a text line with the text tool or insert copied text. Duplicate the text lines (⌘⌥D). Select a text line and a wavy line. **2** Now select the command "Text → Attach To Path" (⌘⇧Y). The position of the text on the path can be altered with the small triangle. To separate the text from the path again select "Text → Detach From Path". For further lines select a line and a text object each time and then apply the above command. If you wish to position text in two semi-circles, as in the example, the text must be separated by a line break (⏎).

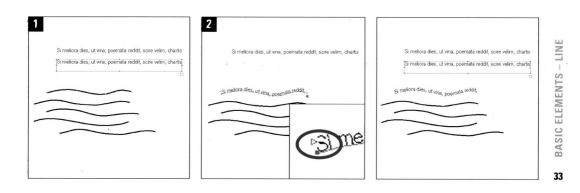

In QuarkXPress produce three compositions from various long lines of the same thickness, decreasing in number: **1** Open an A4 page. Open a square frame and in it some horizontal guidelines at irregular intervals. Drag a 1 pt vertical line the length of the gap up to the first guideline. **2** Duplicate this line with a horizontal offset of 1 mm via the command "Object → Step and Repeat" until the whole width of the page is filled. **3** Drag a further 1 pt vertical line between the first and second guidelines. Again duplicate it until it covers the whole width. **4** Continue like this until the whole square is filled. **5** Now begin the actual design work. Delete individual lines until you have the first powerful composition. **6** Then select all (⌘A on the active Item Tool) and duplicate once with sufficient offset. Remove further lines. **7** Repeat step 6 for the third composition.

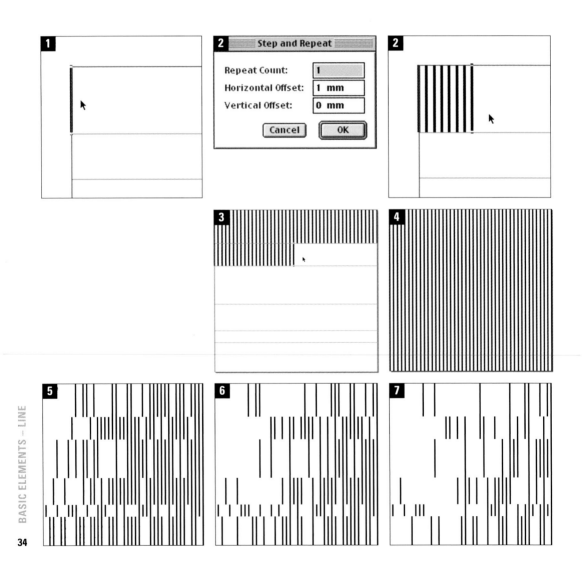

Create 6 text lines in square planes. In the first square put one letter (or a number) per line, in the second square two letters per line, in the third square three letters per line until the latter is completely filled.

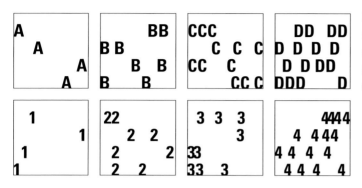

Progression, a variant of rhythm, means growth. Design elements increase in number, size, strength and other parameters. Progression can follow mathematical rules or be intuitive.

Through the changing of parameters a word copied and inserted repeatedly within a square plane should be so designed that an overall rhythmic effect is created. These parameters can be as follows: letter spacing, word spacing, line spacing, number, position, font, font face (bold, italic), font size, rotation. Do not use too many different parameters. In doing the rhythm exercise try to take into account the statement the words are making and visualise this through an appropriate design.

From a formal point of view letters are linear, that is two-dimensional structures. In this exercise the shape details of various letters will be used to divide a square base powerfully into lines. **1** Create a square plane in Freehand. Then with a relatively large font size type a letter with the "Text" tool. **2** Apply the command "Text → Convert to Paths" – so that the letter can be used like a Freehand object. Group the letter (⌘ G). **3** In the colour-field palette put "None" as a fill for the letter and "Black" for the line (stroke). **4** Move the letter above the square and change the size until you are satisfied with the result. **5** Copy the letter on to the clipboard (⌘ C) and select the rectangle. **6** Select the command "Edit → Paste inside". **7** If you want to correct the position retrospectively click on the small blue cross and relocate. If it is the letter itself you want to alter, e.g. line thickness or colour, click the letter with the Alt key (⌥) pressed. To remove the letter from the square again select the square and use the command "Edit → Cut Contents".

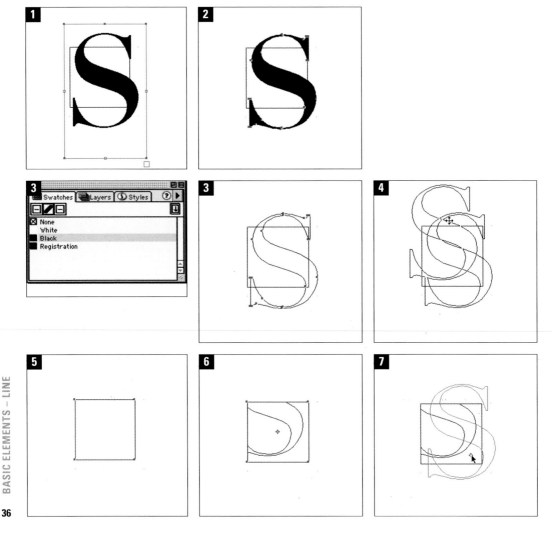

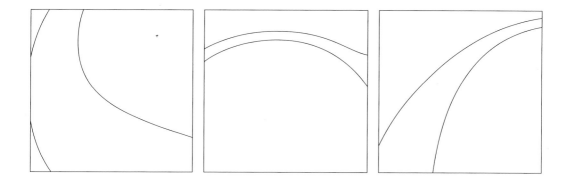

OVERVIEW – LAYING OUT SHAPES

A rectangular space can be divided by arranging individual shapes within it. The arrangement can appear linear, flat or 3-dimensional.

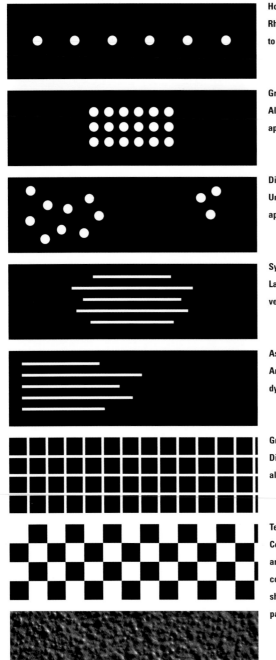

Horizontally aligned

Rhythmic repetition of individual elements (the distance can vary) to form a linear shape

Grouped/Compressed

Aligning of individual elements to form a homogeneous group – appears static

Dispersed/Scattered

Uneven distribution of individual elements on the rectangle – appears dynamic

Symmetry

Laterally reversed arrangement of individual elements along a vertical and horizontal axis – appears static

Asymmetry

Arrangement of individual elements ranged left – appears dynamic

Grid

Divides an area into even parts and is a special form of structure; also used as a principle to order and plan for landscape design

Texture/Structure/Pattern

Composition of a structure through inner order or by shape; there are optically comprehensible surface structures and haptically comprehensible material textures. With the latter, light and shadow are an important factor for the intensity of perception; patterns are created by evenly aligning structural elements

OVERVIEW – EFFECTS OF SHAPES

Elementary shapes that form the basis of almost all 2- or 3-dimensional formations cause certain moods and feelings within us. According to our spatial experiences and habits of seeing, formal structures communicate different formal progressions.

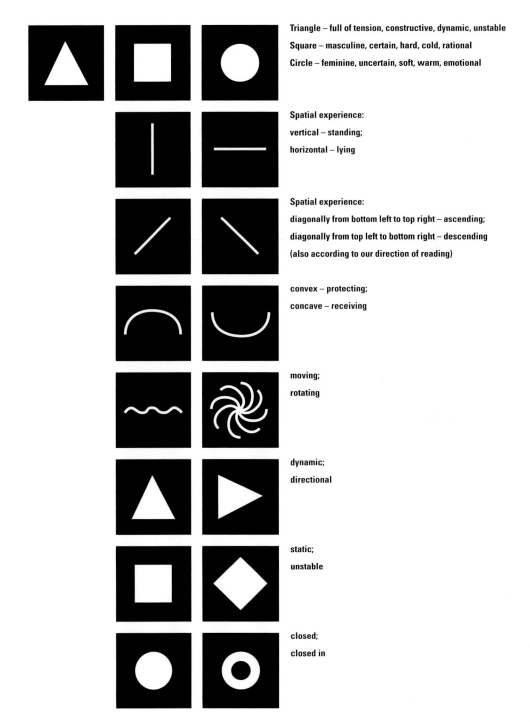

Triangle – full of tension, constructive, dynamic, unstable

Square – masculine, certain, hard, cold, rational

Circle – feminine, uncertain, soft, warm, emotional

Spatial experience:

vertical – standing;

horizontal – lying

Spatial experience:

diagonally from bottom left to top right – ascending;

diagonally from top left to bottom right – descending

(also according to our direction of reading)

convex – protecting;

concave – receiving

moving;

rotating

dynamic;

directional

static;

unstable

closed;

closed in

COMBINATORICS PRINCIPLE OF ORDER – PERMUTATION

Combination theory is an opportunity to configure a restricted number of individual elements in different ways in a complete complex and thereby create new structural shapes. The procedures used can be constructive-systematic or even intuitive. The more complex and numerous the individual elements, the more diverse the structures. Depending on the configuration (see example in the exercises) – despite the same individual elements – the variants produce different structural shapes, which trigger completely different associations. Combination theory is very suitable for designing character systems or character sequences, quite apart from the particular pleasure afforded by experimenting with it. With so-called permutation different structural shapes are created by transposing individual elements from a given supply within the complete complex.

EXERCISE

In the following permutation exercise you can – if you proceed systematically – develop 24 various structural shapes without repetition (1 x 2 x 3 x 4 = 24) from four given individual elements. **1** Set the grid at 10 mm in Freehand ("View → Grid → Edit…/Show/Snap To grid"). Produce a circle 20 x 20 mm. Keep the grouping (⌘ ⇧ G). **2** Set the knife tool as illustrated below. Then on the selected circle drag the knife tool once horizontally and once vertically through the marking points. Then immediately clear the selection (→|). **3** Now you can click the elements individually and move them. **4** As backup the four parts can be identified by the letters a, b, c, and d. A letter is grouped with each part (because of the exact positioning take care that the letter is positioned inside the arc). Clone each of the four parts and relocate them as in the patterns on the opposite page. Finally the letters can be deleted and a square frame applied to each shape.

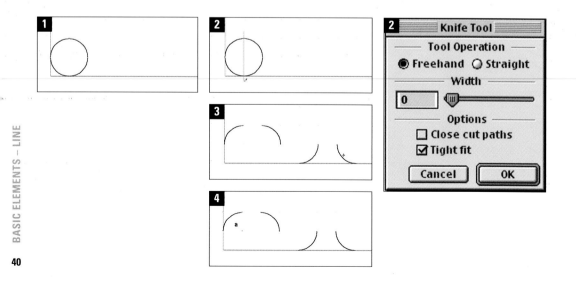

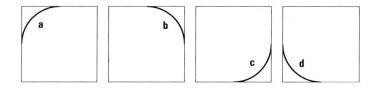

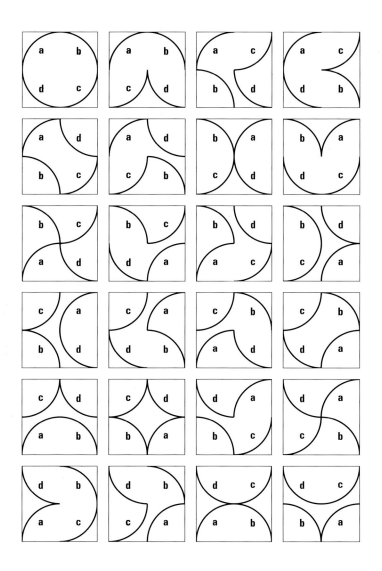

COMBINATORICS PRINCIPLE OF ORDER – SUPER CHARACTERS

A result of permutation can be so-called super characters. These are complex characters built up from several composite individual characters. A super character is formed from a basic shape which is altered by repetition, rotation (for example by 90%) and variation. There are numerous options for designing super characters.

EXERCISE For the following combination theory exercise use a basic element as well as three variants of it, which are each rotated by 90, 180 and 270 degrees. **1** In Freehand design a square plane of 7.5 x 7.5 mm with 3 angled lines. For this set the grid at 2.5 mm ("View → Grid → Edit…/Show/Snap To grid"). **2** Select the drawing pen and set the "Paintbrush" option as displayed. **3** Draw the lines, keeping the shift key (⇧) pressed for horizontal or vertical lines. Group the three angles. **4** Clone the group (⌘ ⇧ D) and shift it by 10 mm. Then rotate the group by 90% with the aid of the "Transformation" palette. **5** Repeat step 4 twice. **6** Draw a rectangle 22.5 x 22.5 as a border line for the super characters, duplicate 24 times and distribute the duplicates evenly over the page. Now assemble separate groups of 3 x 3 individual elements by cloning and relocating the required elements. The grid provides a good way of doing this. Try to design interesting and diverse structural shapes. In the next step you will be able to develop your own basic shapes and develop from them more super characters. Try to conjure up associations for them or conversely try to develop super characters for particular sensations.

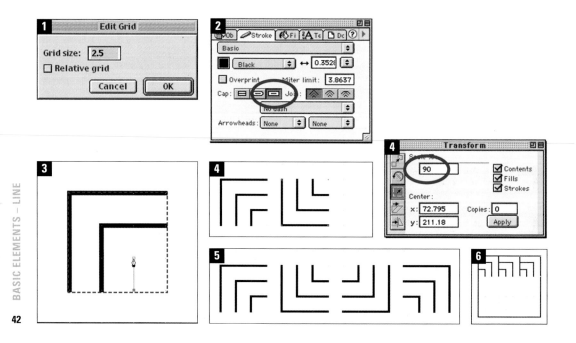

COMBINATORICS – SUPER CHARACTERS – CONTINUOUS DESIGN

A continuation of combination theory allows us to create quick representational, ornamental and decorative structural shapes (circles or angles) out of initially abstract basic shapes. Continuous patterns, also called repeating patterns, can be produced very simply from the super characters once they have been designed. The essential feature of the continuous pattern – regular repetition – has already been created in the super character. Should the continuous pattern become more complex, then the super character can be enlarged by increasing the number of individual elements, e.g. from 3 x 3 individual elements to 4 x 4.

EXERCISE

1 In Freehand copy a super character from the previous exercises (without frames) into a new document. Select all ([⌘] A) and ungroup the object ([⌘] [⇧] G). Copy on to the clipboard ([⌘] C). **2** Draw a new rectangle and leave it marked. Select "Window → Inspectors → Fill…" and then the option "Page Frame". **3** Now click the program switch "One" (insert). The clipboard's content will be inserted as filling and the marked object filled with the pattern. **4** The size and position of the pattern in this palette can however be changed.

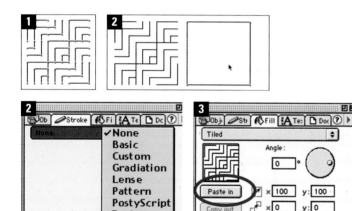

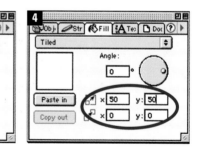

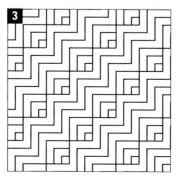

Basis for the patterns are 2 x four permutations from page 41

1

1 "Drawing Of A Two Year Old Child" (Gemma Lewandowsky).
2 Morgan O'Hara, "Portraits and Worlds", 1981–1983, diverse
techniques. (Printed by kind permission of the artist.)
3 Nanne Meyer, from the series "Seidemar. Kataster", 2002,
14.8 x 10 cm. (Printed by kind permission of the artist.)

Lines serve to represent paths. At the same time each line is a
piece of documented movement. Morgan O'Hara presents the
paths people have trodden in their lifetime, such as journeys or
moves, which she has recorded in cartographic diagrams.
Nanne Meyer redraws maps and weather charts she has
discovered and suchlike. The child's drawing displays the
dynamic and characteristic style with which the distance of a
line on paper is covered.

2

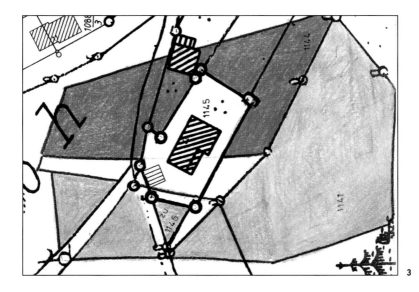

3

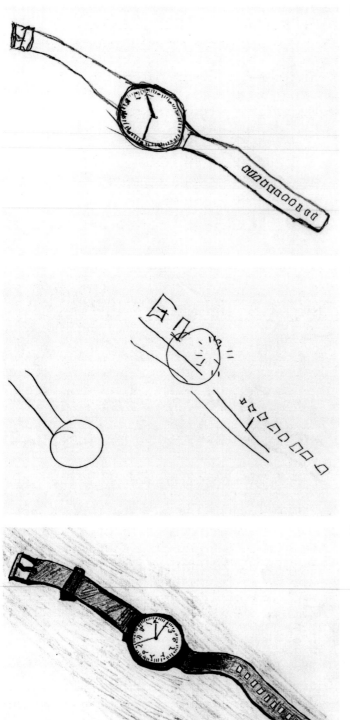

Drawing "by heart" as outline

Drawing "blind"

Three-dimensional drawing

DRAWING, DRAWING, DRAWING...

Drawing teaches you to see. To convey observation in a two-dimensional drawing presupposes a high level capacity for abstraction. This is not simply an ability that some people have and others don't. It is a process of experience which starts with being prepared to undertake persistent conscious observation. This process can of course only be experienced by those who take the time to draw. Having talent consists mainly of summoning up interest and full attention for seeing as drawing. Persevering with drawing objects, landscapes, people and animals – at rest or moving, in various formats and on various bases – is a basic exercise for all those with any visual interest; through it one gradually acquires the ability to design in the abstract and to recognise visual codes as well. Being able not only to decipher abstract characters or compositions but also to design them follows from the basic drawing exercise. It is such endeavours that spark off creative freedom.

"The base for a drawing is the paper.

The paper is the scope for a drawing.

The playing field is as white as its base.

The white is the void that surrounds everything.

The format shows the white its limits.

The white is the field for the eyes.

The field of vision is a feast for the eyes, which blurs towards the edges.

The paper is boundary and clarity, drawing is surplus and doubt.

Together this means: deviate, give space to the unexpected, the unforeseen."

(Nanne Meyer)

NOT WITHOUT MANUAL ROUGH SKETCHES

In what way can drawing contribute to the visual handling of DTP programs on the computer? Drawing forms the basis for the organising of pictorial objects on the plane. It is the quintessential basis for composition of professional visual design and of its assessment as of every other artistic/visual form of expression. Drawing teaches you to see. A casually scribbled "visual reflection" on a piece of paper often intuitively leads to a compositionally satisfactory solution or forms the starting point, premise and theme for design work on the computer. The computer should remain an aid. So that you don't lose yourself in the jungle of the endless artistic options which the computer offers, you shouldn't begin the layout of an invitation card, for example, without jotting down ideas first. Everywhere the appeal of images overwhelms us like a torrent. If you counter this profusion with a simple, independent attitude whereby you develop your own criteria, it will allow you to select from the abundant choice on offer and you won't then be distracted by every cheap tool that is offered you.

SEEING OBJECTS – DRAWING OBJECTS

"What is there to see? First of all the obvious things, the small things, the minutiae in my immediate vicinity that catch my eye. Like an 'ostinato of the ordinary' they permeate my drawings: pins and needles, a piece of soap, brushes and bristles, a light bulb, a whisk, perhaps a bit of butter, books, items of clothing, paper patterns, shoes and soles…" (Meyer). Find a familiar object that you encounter every day. Invest in a sketchbook and in it draw the object from various perspectives. First draw the object in outline, then three-dimensionally with shading, then with your left hand, then from memory and also with different writing and drawing implements. Draw the object in different localities. Draw an overall view, then just a detail of it. In this way you gain your own collection of visual material which you can incidentally continue working on at the computer. When drawing from nature begin with a soft pencil. A pencil helps you proceed slowly, to feel for the object's dimensions with tentative, delicate strokes, to hint at its details, in order gradually to tease out its substance. Fine drawing pens are good for scribbling layout sketches and the position of lettering in a format. Thus in time you discover your preferences and preferred aids.

The process of drawing is a translation process: The drawing of a house is not a house but a drawing. Wishing to make a "proper" drawing is often a hindrance. Try to free yourself from the constructs of professional standards and expectations. Understand drawing as a playful, unacademic process for setting free your creative energies, as a searching for design possibilities. The result can well be an incomplete "not proper" drawing. Don't be afraid of failing. Drawing takes practice and that takes time.

DRAWING Find an object that is small, portable, expressive (in its form) and commonly known. Draw in a notebook or on sketching paper which you can later file into a folder. It is worth keeping the drawings.

1 Put the object on the table and draw it:
– as a formal drawing (as exact as possible), three-dimensional and with drop shadow
– as line drawing (only outline, no contours)
– two-dimensional only with surface structure
– from various perspectives
– with only one line, simplifying the object and reducing it to its essence.

2 Put the object on the table and look at it for seven minutes. Then cover it up and try to draw it "by heart".

3 Put the object on the table and look at it for seven minutes. Then close your eyes and draw it "blindly".

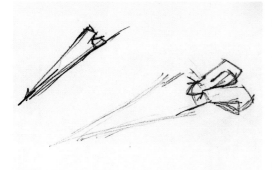

Drawing "blind"

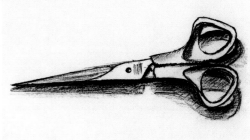

Three-dimensional drawing

Linear drawing

Two-dimensional drawing

4 Put the object on the table and draw it in its spatial context, i.e. in front of different backgrounds.

5 Draw an object with attributes: sad, cheerful, fast, slow, hard, soft.

6 Draw stories with your object in the title role. When drawing, develop a storyboard or scenes of a cartoon animation.

Repeat these exercises after a while with different objects or the same object and compare the results. Keep drawing.

DRAWINGS, PATHS, ORIENTATION

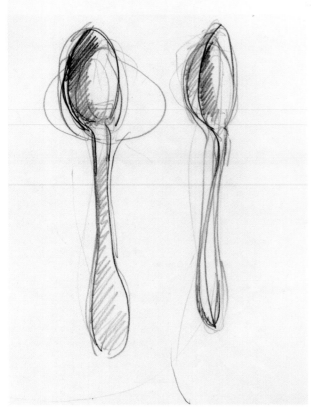

Francis Zeischegg, Sketches from "Messer, Gabel, Löffel" (Knife, Fork, Spoon), 1985.

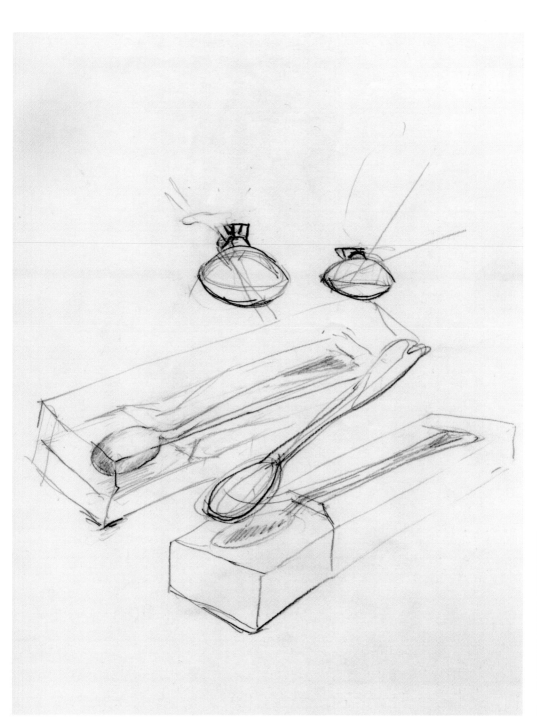

Francis Zeischegg, Sketches from
"Messer, Gabel, Löffel – Einsamer Löffel"
(Knife, Fork, Spoon – Lonely Spoon), 1985.

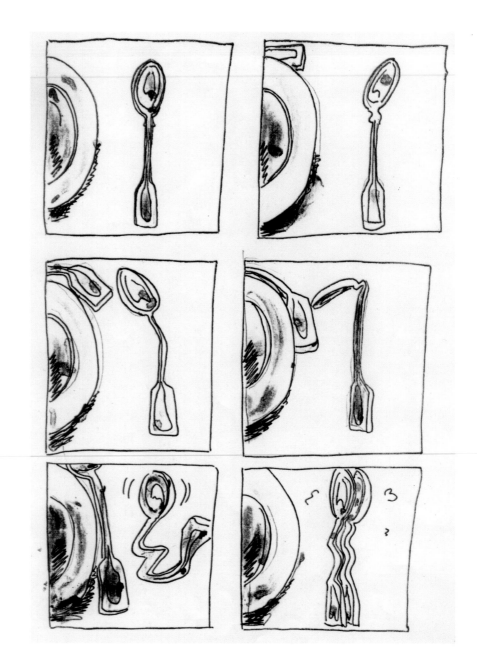

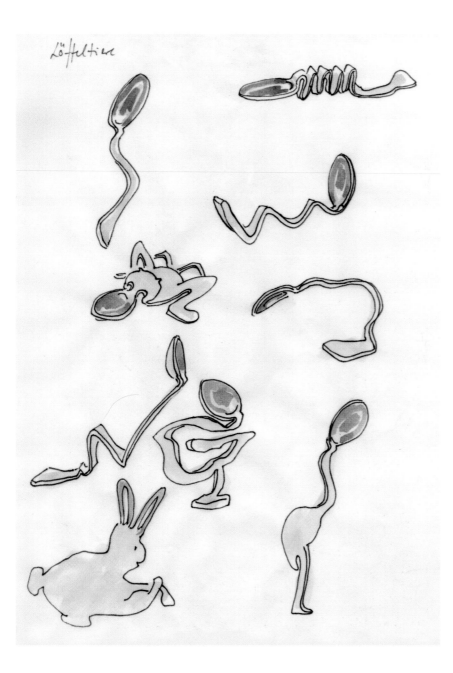

Löffeltier

PRINCIPLES OF ANIMATION

In principle, cartoon animation is the drawing of an element that consists of several parts which are then copied and changed by fractions. In a hand drawing like "Verlegenheit" (Embarrassment) the figure has to be manually drawn a few times and then subtly changed for each emotion. The computer helps enormously with this kind of work. A copy of the picture on the left was created in QuarkXPress; all parts were then grouped together and duplicated a few times. In this way, the minimal changes – shown in red – were easily achievable. Following this principle, try to create a "cartoon animation", using the most simple figures or day-to-day objects.

Drawing as a game – children's drawings "Kellervermassung" (measuring the cellar). Ten year old David Neuhaus and Samy Lankisch draw floor plans of various basements after having surveyed the locations.

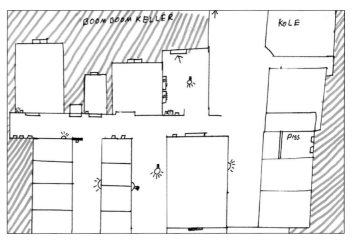

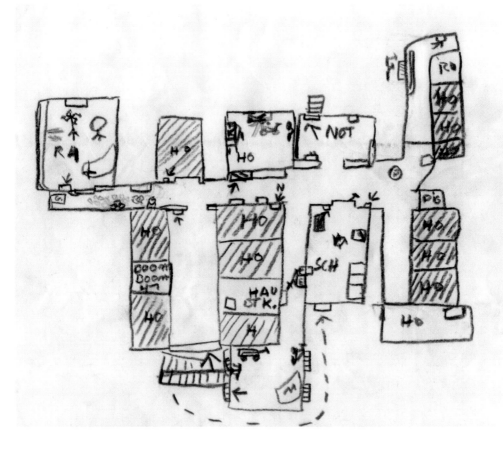

City map and game plan

PATHS, PLANS, ORIENTATION

Signs and colour markings in the street or on a map help us to spatially orientate ourselves. "The orientation map is a schematic graphic of a more or less certain reality, which for man today has ceased to be understandable in its spatial and temporal dimensions. (…) For us, the word 'map' in this context means a visual division of a space or temporal process (game plan). Structure or subdivision are schematic principles on which something is ordered or happens," (Frutiger).

"Orientation": map drawings are lined up due north

© **Student work by Markus Grellert**

A linear route map is to be created in a square (13 x 13 cm). For instance, try from memory to visualise your route from home to work. Draw two or three possible routes: on foot, by public transport, by bicycle or car. If your home is also your place of work, find other succinct routes – it can for instance be the route from your bed to your desk or a favourite walking route.

1a Make yourself aware of the most important landmarks and sketch them along the route by drawing spots and labelling them accordingly and connect them with a simple line. You can also copy the route from a road map with the help of tracing paper and a fine drawing pen. **1b** Alternatively, you can redraw the detail of your road map in Photoshop in a new layer (create a layer in between with a white fill and reduce the opacity). Create simple geometrical symbols for start, finish, railway stations, or other useful places (spot, line, square, triangle, cross or amorphous symbols, as outline or silhouette). Create a legend. On the plan, define the four points of the compass (orientation). In this way you can describe a direction geographically.

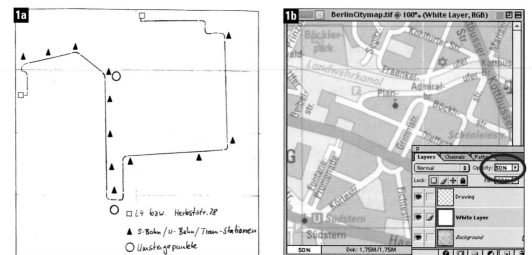

2 Create the same route map in Freehand with the drawing or line tool. To construct the route system, it is advisable to switch on the grid ("View → Grid → Show/ Snap To Grid"). **3** You can also construct the geometrical shapes in Freehand. Reacquaint yourself with the impact hierarchy of geometrical symbols. Which symbol is in the foreground, which symbol is in the background (see page 14). **4** Structure your cartographical work by importance, using varying thicknesses of lines and dots. Duplicate the symbols and assign them to the individual landmarks on the map. **5** Again create another legend. **6** Print the map and compare it to your drawing. Is the digitally created map of better legibility than the drawing? What are the advantages of the drawing? What would you want to improve? Present your map to friends and examine whether they can read and understand it.

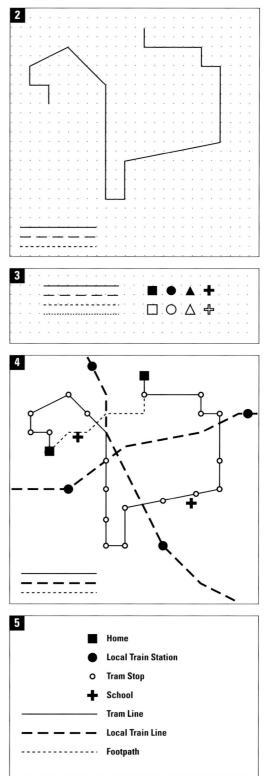

Home
Local Train Station
Tram Stop
School
Tram Line
Local Train Line
Footpath

Example: legend

1

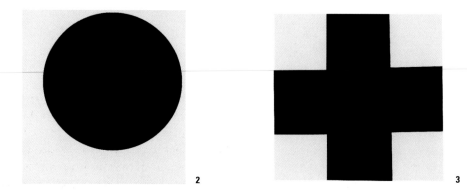

2

3

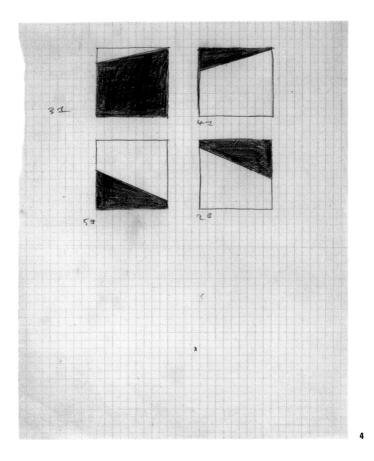

4

1 Kazimir Malevich, "Schwarzes Quadrat" (Black Square), circa 1927, oil on canvas, 106 x 106 cm.
2 Kazimir Malevich, "Schwarzer Kreis" (Black Circle), circa 1927, oil on canvas, 105 x 105 cm.
3 Kazimir Malevich, "Schwarzes Kreuz" (Black Cross), circa 1927, oil on canvas, 106 x 106 cm.
4 François Morellet, "Studie" (Study), 1958, pencil on checked paper, 9 x 21 cm.
(Printed by kind permission of the artists.)

In this chapter, in order to gain experience working with the basic design element "plane", we position square planes on white backgrounds. Today this seems self-evident. In 1920s' Moscow, Kazimir Malevich caused a revolution in the art world when he painted a large-format "black square" in oils. It was the first time an artist deemed the most simple geometric shapes worthy to be subjects for a painting. Subsequently, geometric shapes became a timeless subject of artistic examination, as with François Morellet's work.

PLANE DIVISION AND PROPORTIONS

One of the most essential design factors is the determination of proportions. Proportions are the relations between sizes, as well as luminosity or between colours. Tension is created with a well-proportioned or well-divided plane. A balanced weighting gives a work of design artistic persuasion. We recognise the free division, the halving division (for example with DIN-formats) and the "golden section" (a ratio of 1 : 1,618) as the basic ways of proportioning. After the important question of format (also see page 67), the second important decision to be made with each layout or poster design is the division of the plane. Not only is it a question of size relationships between one element and the plane, but also relationships between individual elements including their distance and position. We arrive at the question as to which components should be used on the plane, and which axis should images, typography and blocks of text follow. As well as a well-balanced format – the best possible ratio between width and height – you can also determine a powerful division of the plane, on which a horizontal and a vertical line cross each other, with comparative testing using movable black angles (see page 11). In this way relations of forms can be created and made visible.

Square

Portrait

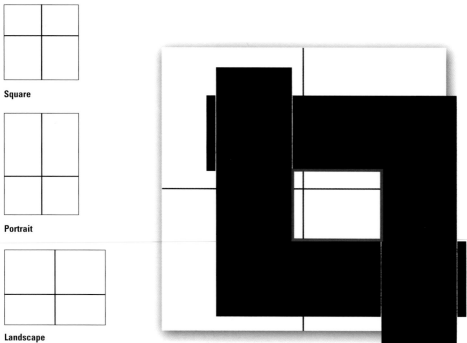

Landscape

EXERCISE   The same exercise on the computer: On an A4 page, for instance in QuarkXPress, open a page-sized picture frame and fill it in with black. Create six white squares. Pull a horizontal and vertical line across each square and arrange them in a way that is interesting and full of tension (see facing page).

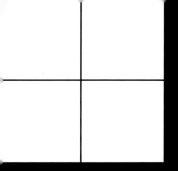

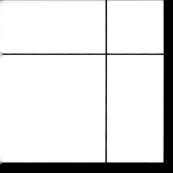
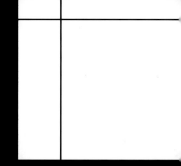
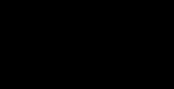
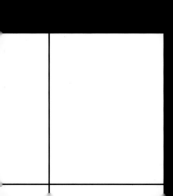
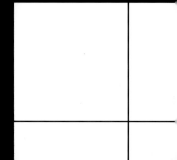

EXERCISE Convert the axis compositions into plane compositions created in the previous exercise. Open four picture frames on top of your first axis composition and give each a different fill colour. Duplicate these four frames and move over your next composition. Change the frame ratios and size but keep the colour in order to compare the different plane arrangements. This exercise gives you a basic orientation with layout concepts.

LAYOUT SCRIBBLE – HAND-DRAWN SKETCH

If you design for print, you have various images, texts and an idea of how many and which colours you want to work with. The solution does not happen in your head nor on your computer. **1** Open a page in any format with a few empty picture frames in a layout program and print a few copies. Draw a horizontal and vertical line in each of them and thus determine the centre of gravity. **2** Into the so created fields sketch the elements that make up the content of your design projects (illustrations, text, colour panels or headlines). The axes can either be used as borders between two fields or outer perimeters for text lines or imagery. Top and bottom margins of a headline, if aligned to an axis, stabilise the overall design. Learn more about this in the chapter "Modular Constructions".

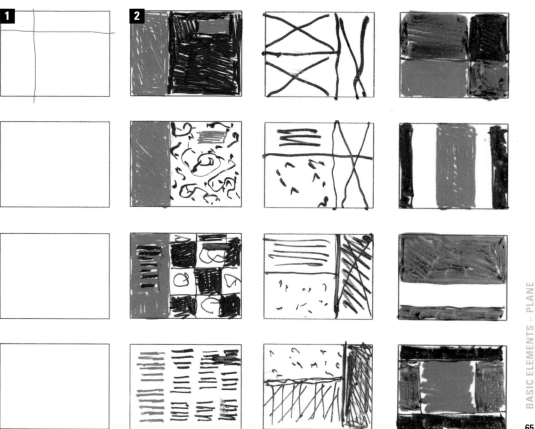

THE FORMAT

To begin the design process we need a format, a basic plane (we will discuss the plane as a design element later in the book). Every plane is a certain size and is limited to a certain shape – with a sheet of paper or this book the trim edges are the format limits. The plane can also be a newspaper column or a 48-sheet billboard. The format is determined by a definite height/width ratio. Accordingly, we differentiate between portrait, landscape or square format. The decision of which format to use almost always happens at the start of the design process and is closely related to the intended communication. The choice of format can also be related to budget or dictated measurements – but within these limits it shouldn't be of our concern.

EXERCISE   To understand which format is most suited to which design task, you can fill in the following polarity profiles. Let also other "experimenters" fill in these forms in order to compare notes. Find suitable examples for three different formats.

Polarity profile portrait format

	1	0	1	
high				low
weak				strong
active				passive
small				big
young				old
tense				relaxed
sad				happy
fresh				stale
near				far
unstable				stable
progressive				conservative

Polarity profile square format

	1	0	1	
high				low
weak				strong
active				passive
small				big
young				old
tense				relaxed
sad				happy
fresh				stale
near				far
unstable				stable
progressive				conservative

Polarity profile landscape format

	1	0	1	
high				low
weak				strong
active				passive
small				big
young				old
tense				relaxed
sad				happy
fresh				stale
near				far
unstable				stable
progressive				conservative

	1	0	1	
high	x			low
weak		x		strong
active	x			passive
small		x		big
young	x			old
tense	x			relaxed
sad		x		happy
fresh	x			stale
near	x			far
unstable		x		stable
progressive		x		conservative

	1	0	1	
high		x		low
weak		x		strong
active	x			passive
small			x	big
young		x		old
tense		x		relaxed
sad		x		happy
fresh		x		stale
near		x		far
unstable			x	stable
progressive		x		conservative

	1	0	1	
high			x	low
weak		x		strong
active			x	passive
small		x		big
young			x	old
tense			x	relaxed
sad	x			happy
fresh			x	stale
near			x	far
unstable			x	stable
progressive			x	conservative

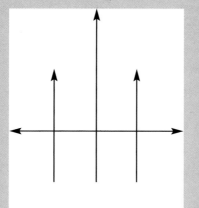

Portrait format doesn't appear neutral, but upright, as well as ascending and hence active. It suggests growth, reaching for the light, standing up. It is the most commonly used format of all.

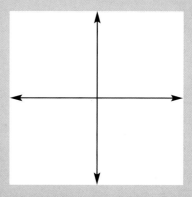

Through even proportions, the square format appears neutral, calm, well-balanced and unmoved. Both directions of motion (horizontal and vertical) are equal.

Landscape format does not appear neutral, but reclining, oppressive and hence passive and heavy. It suggests inner peace, something flowing and horizontal motion.

RELATIONSHIP BETWEEN ELEMENTS AND THE BACKGROUND

As with a dot and line, each shape structure behaves in a certain way in relation to the basic plane it sits on. A circular shape differs in behaviour from an angular shape, inner form from outer form (see also page 95), a vertical rectangle from a square. There is a serious difference between showing the whole object on the plane, or only a cropped detail and of course the format plays a decisive role. In every case it is a question of a more or less vibrant division of the plane, a composition in which shape and background play equal roles. Elements arranged on a plane exist in relation to their surrounding space, the outer limits of which are represented by its edges. This surrounding space or background in turn forms a shape in itself, a formal structure which behaves proportionally to the whole plane. Each minimal alteration of position, size, shape, brightness or colour of a single element brings about a change in the background. Again take some time here to work through the exercises on the following pages and even additional ones. Also try to verbally define the visual impressions (e.g. it appears large/small, near/far, thick/thin). In so doing, you grow accustomed to the programs as well as acquire valuable viewing experience, which trains you in dealing with more discriminative image-linguistic elements. You are already familiar with the technique of creating a new document in Freehand or QuarkXPress, with opening object frames and defining fill and stroke and with creating additional objects to arrange on the plane (also see page 16).

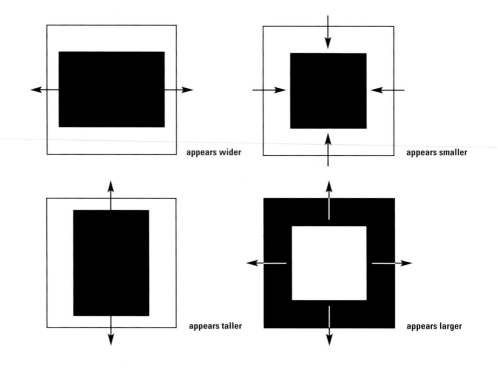

appears wider

appears smaller

appears taller

appears larger

BASIC ELEMENTS – PLANE

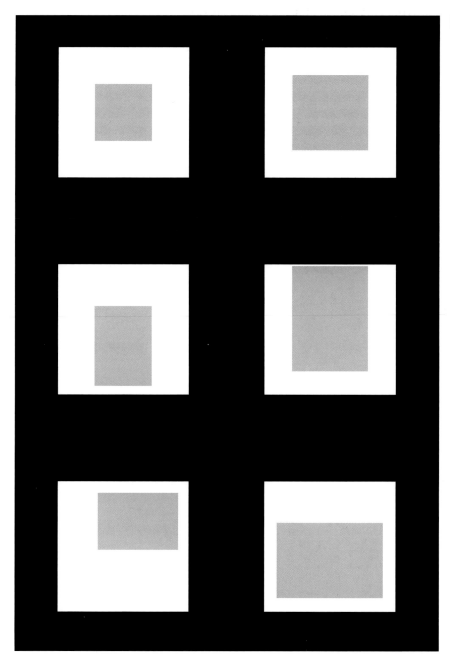

Open a new A4 document. As background, create a page-filling frame with black fill. Open six white squares (80 x 80 mm) and arrange them evenly. In each of these square planes position one of these three formal structures: square, vertical rectangle and horizontal rectangle. Give these objects a grey fill (30% black) and vary the object sizes. Find interesting positions in the format and pay attention to the effect of the shape (see also page 39).

BASIC ELEMENTS – PLANE

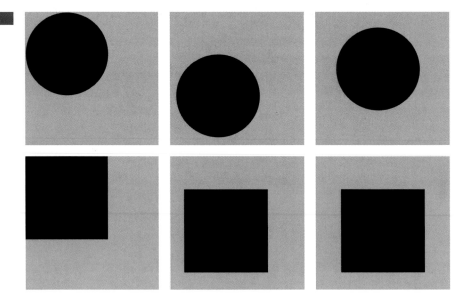

Create a new A4 document or modify the document from the previous exercise. Use the six evenly arranged squares as basic planes and give them a grey fill (30% black). Create geometrical black shapes (circle 65 x 65 mm, square 60 x 60 mm) as shown in the illustration above. Now position one black object on each of the squares. Visualise the terms: calm, restless, focused, happy, sad, bored. Create captions with the terms in legible type size underneath. And here again, distance yourself from your work by arranging prints on the floor to look at them from a standing position.

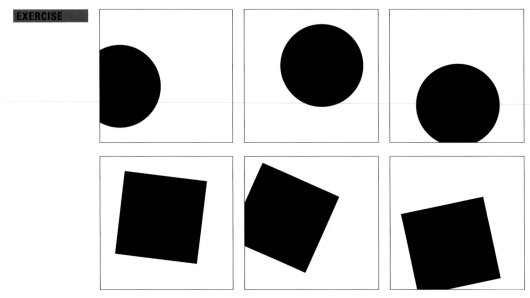

This next exercise is best achieved in Freehand (illustration opposite page, bottom). **1** Create six evenly distributed basic squares (80 x 80 mm) with a black outline. Position one black shape (circle 65 x 65 mm, square 60 x 60 mm) on each of them by cropping into the basic square, but only far enough for the black shape to still be recognisable. **2** Once you are satisfied with the position, keep the black shape selected and use the command "Edit → Cut (⌘X)". Now select the background square and use the command "Edit → Paste Inside (⌘⇧V)". If you want to correct the position of the black square subsequently, click on the small blue cross and move again. Incidentally, a rotated square shape ("Windows → Panels → Transform: Rotate") is more likely to be recognised as a square if presented as a detail. Cropping into a shape aligned horizontally or vertically easily results in a rectangle. **3** Duplicate the individual frames containing the positioned black objects and select the square container. Fill the "newly created figure" with a colour and examine the black shape for harmonious and vibrant positioning on the background.

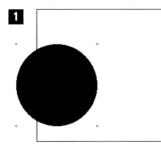

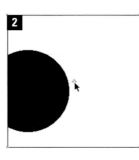

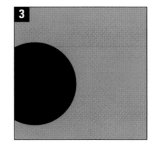

Create a new document in Freehand. Create two different basic planes: two squares, two vertical rectangles and two horizontal rectangles each with a black outline. Position a black circle in each of these format frames **1** uncropped on the plane and **2** cropped on the plane and assign them each to one of the descriptive terms mentioned on the previous page. Complete the same exercise with a square. Which format is most suited in relation to the form. Again give the background a colour fill and examine the proportions.

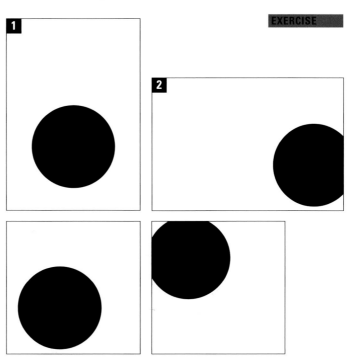

EXERCISE Design three exercise sheets with individually differing plane compositions on nine basic square backgrounds (50 x 50 mm) with overlapping black squares. Choose the number of squares at will. On the first sheet (examples in the first row) work with equally sized black squares (23 x 23 mm) – and again on the second sheet but here you can also rotate the squares (examples in the second row). On the third sheet use squares of differing sizes (5, 10, 15, 20 and 25 mm) to design the compositions (examples in the third row). Pay attention to the interaction between figure and background.

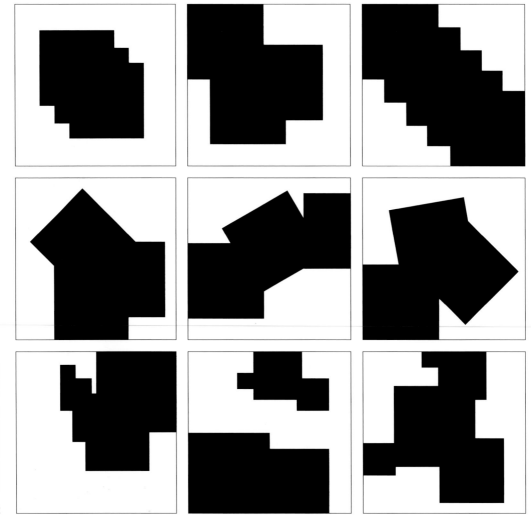

COMBINATORICS PRINCIPLE OF ORDER – VARIATION

When dividing and laying out a plane, instead of working intuitively one can also work constructively and systematically. This is achieved with the help of the combinatorics principle. Individual elements, limited to a few shapes, are arranged into a new unit and thus create a new form structure. The simplest way of combinatorics is variation. Try to deconstruct the example below. The basis here are two individual elements, the second of which is a 180° rotated version of the first. You can also use the two elements shown on the right. By arranging four individual elements with the help of duplication into a square, a new unit is constructed with these two elements. As you can see, even with such a limited number of individual elements it is possible to create an infinite number of new structures. The more complex and numerous the individual elements, the more varied the result (also see page 40).

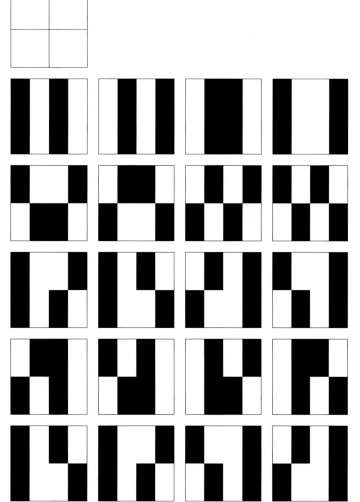

OVERVIEW – CONTRASTS OF SHAPE

Contrasts develop between two adjacent forms. Similar shapes weaken each other – conflicting shapes disassociate themselves from each other. The clearer the difference between two forms, the stronger the conflict.

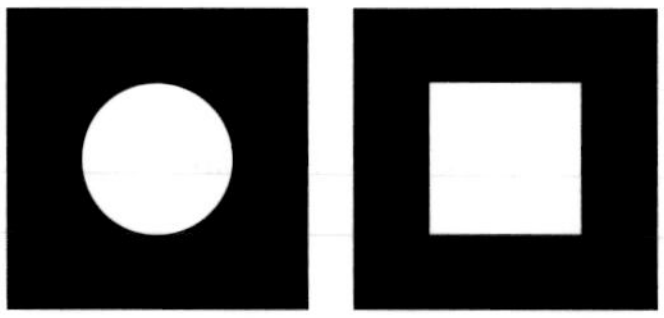

Shape-contrast

The basic geometrical shapes create

the simplest and at the same time

strongest contrast

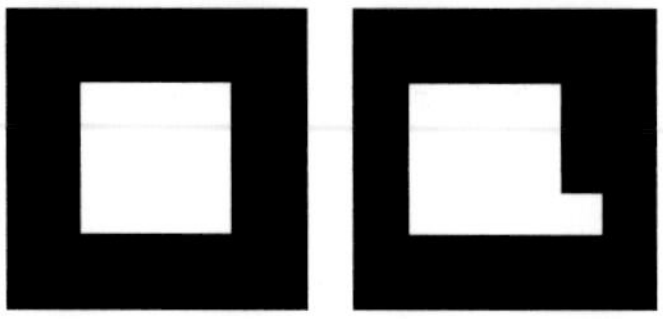

Quality contrast

Opposition of even and uneven shapes

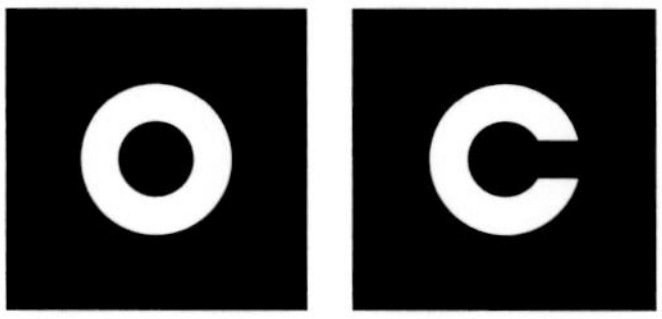

Quality contrast

Opposition of closed and open forms

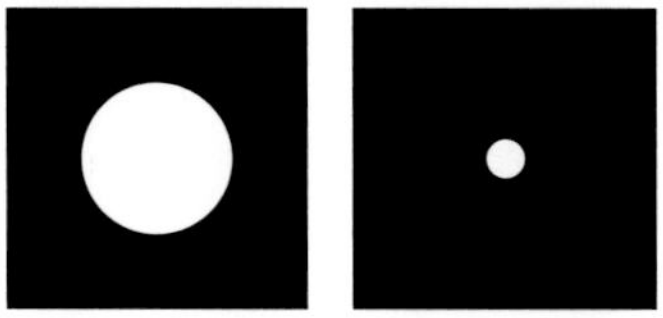

Quantity contrast

Contrast between dimensions of form,

e. g. large – small

Quantity contrast

Contrast between dimensions of form,

e. g. wide – narrow

Directional contrast

Direction – opposite direction;

ascending – falling;

up – down

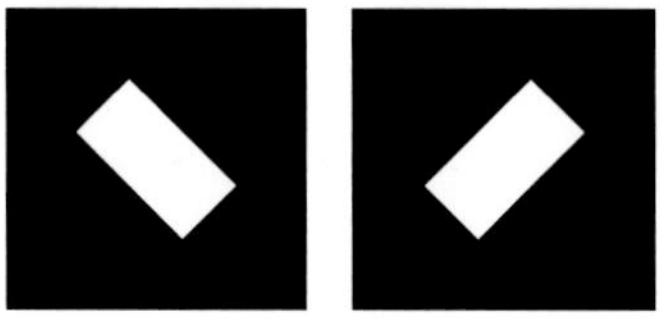

Directional contrast

Direction – opposite direction;

vibration – anti-vibration;

to – fro

OVERVIEW – RELATIONSHIPS BETWEEN SHAPES

Form relationships are created by differing arrangements of forms on a plane. Form relationships are the key to expression and effect.

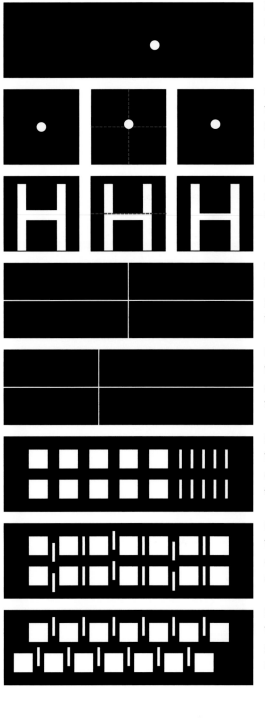

Development of centre of gravity

Form positions on a plane create a centre of gravity. It can be varied depending on the desired message (see page 85).

Optical centre

The geometrical centre is perceived as too low and hence incorrect. This can be corrected by positioning a form slightly higher.

Optical centre

Letters also seem too low when positioned in the geometrical centre.

Format / proportion

Proportion is the relationship between sizes and between the partial to the whole. The halving division, e.g. with DIN-formats is the most commonly used.

Format / golden section

The "golden section" is recognised as the ideal proportion in art and nature, although it is rarely applied correctly. The division ratio is 1 : 1.618.

Contrast

The contrast between several elements happens through effect and arrangement of form. The greater the difference, the stronger the effect.

Rhythm

This is created by repetition and slight variation of form, size and/or position of elements. A rhythmical arrangement is always also a moved order.

Dynamic

This is a perception of motion that can be created through vibrant positioning of elements on a plane – and their individual relationships.

PLANE AND FONT

Letters are distinct elements consisting of individual geometrical forms. For those who are not thoroughly trained as designers, the polished appeal of individual typefaces can be immensely tempting and they are primarily perceived as carriers of cognitive information and only secondarily or never as graphic elements and part of a composition. The capital N of a sans-serif, medium font corresponds with a square shape, the capital O corresponds with a circular shape. Even though letters – through their fragmented inner form – develop stronger contrasts than simple circular or square shapes, they compositionally behave as figures to the plane and develop relationships in accordance. As individual forms, type behaves proportionally to its surroundings. Here we want to examine this fact more closely and thus make ourselves aware of it.

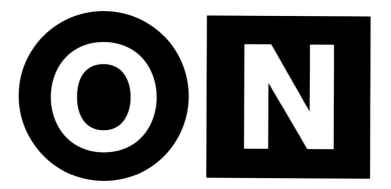

EXERCISE On an A4 document, position two black basic shapes – a square and a circle – in at least three different formats with a grey background (square, vertical and horizontal rectangle).

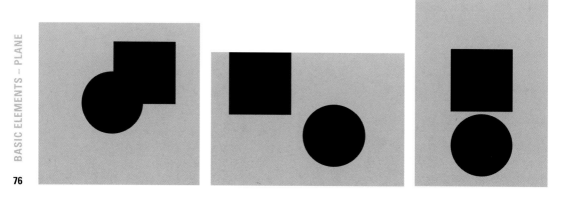

Open a new A4 document. Open a background frame across the whole page and give it a grey fill (30% black). Create six square object frames (50 x 50 mm) with no fill and an outline of 1 pt (⌘B) and distribute them evenly across the page. Into two individual text boxes type the letters **n** and **o** in a medium, sans-serif font (Arial, Helvetica, Frutiger) and set the type size to about 100 pt. In the measurements palette, set the text alignment to "centred" and do this also with the vertical alignment (⌘M). Position the individual letters on the plane as formal elements (what can you read – no or on?). Additionally, visualise the word "no" as well as other short terms according to their meaning in the square.

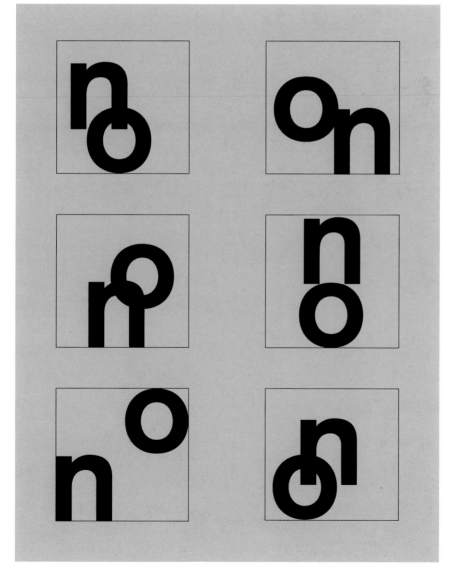

Position the word "no" in relation to the plane on at least three different random formats. Play around with different shades of grey.

On an A4 page in QuarkXPress, create several compositions with the basic geometrical shapes of a square, circle and triangle as well as letters which correspond to these shapes. Use a black shape as background and each time position one white letter of a sans-serif font (Arial, Frutiger, Akzidenz Grotesk – light, medium or bold) on the shape. Try and divide the background with the help of the still recognisable letter as vibrantly as possible. You can combine contrasting and resembling shapes.

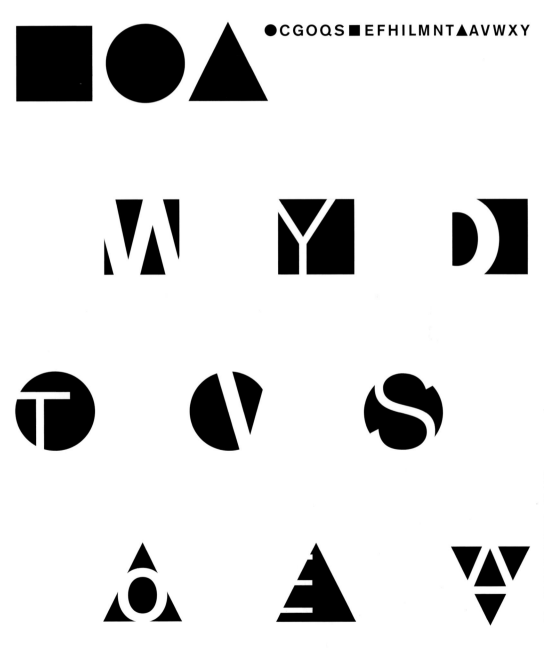

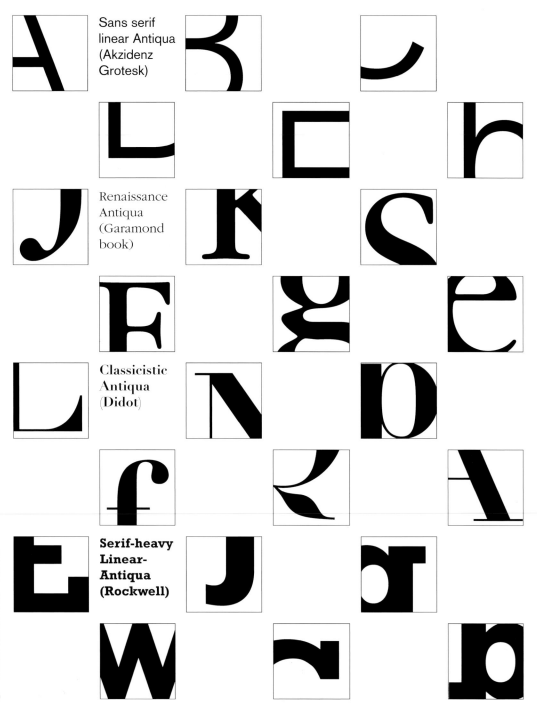

Sans serif
linear Antiqua
(Akzidenz
Grotesk)

Renaissance
Antiqua
(Garamond
book)

**Classicistic
Antiqua
(Didot)**

**Serif-heavy
Linear-
Antiqua
(Rockwell)**

As you have already seen on pages 37 and 79, letter forms are not only symbols which – put together to shape words and letters – communicate information, but also formal design elements. Thus they follow the same formal rules as dot, line and plane. The exercises on this double page spread have the purpose of teaching you how to create vibrant relationships between formal structures and the plane. To start with work with the inner form (see below). At the same time, we want to create sensitivity for the formal qualities of faces from differing type families, by steering your particular attention to typical attributes. Going by the characteristic details of the four different type classes shown on the left, try to find similar typefaces (type classification is consciously not included in this book – it can be read up on in various other books). Also try to hand-draw letters of different type classes (first by copying, later by memory). Thus you can train yourself in dealing with typography. (For more information on this exercise see also page 37.) To cut the inner form in Freehand: **1** Create a letter and convert it into paths by using the command "Text → Convert To Paths". **2** Now use "Modify → Split" and then deselect. **3** Select the outer form (you might have to switch off "Preview" in the "View" menu to see the individual outlines) and delete it. **4** After having pasted the inner shape into the square (Cut the shape, select the square and use "Edit → Paste Inside") it can be selected and moved around by clicking on it with the alt-key pressed down (⊡) (more shapes: also press Shift).

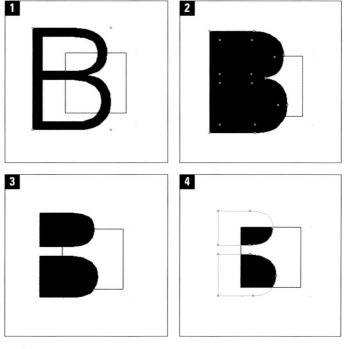

PLANE AND SHAPE

Relationships full of tension between form and plane are also at the heart of this exercise. A simple photographic shape is to be arranged on a square plane. Examine the formal relationship to the background by using different positions, sizes and rotation as well as arranging several equally sized copies on the plane. Scan any small enough object of daily use (simply place it on the scanner) and create a cut-out in Photoshop by using the command "Image → Extract..." and/or by using a layer mask. Then duplicate the layer with the cut-out object several times and create a white layer as background.

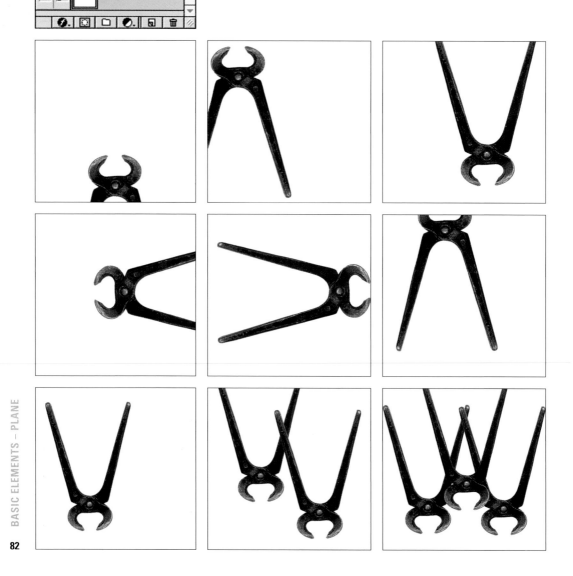

TEXT AS COLUMN

Create a new A4 document with six squares or copy one from a former exercise. Set the words "Fear", "Honour", "Courage" in a separate text frame at a size of between 24 pt to 48 pt in a sans-serif font (Arial, Frutiger, Akzidenz-Grotesk). Choose a medium type style.

For the columns, duplicate each of the text boxes and fill black. Now position the text boxes with the words vibrantly in three of the squares. Now arrange the black text boxes in the other three squares in corresponding positions. Like this you have the possibility to analyse each chosen text position on the background and examine its relationship with the surrounding space.

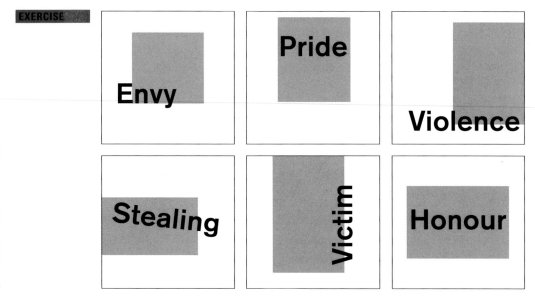

In another A4 document arrange a further six square frames with black outlines (opposite page, bottom). You can now put the individual typographical units (terms) in relation to different, rectangular grey shapes (see also pages 69–70). Try to express the meaning of each word when designing the formal relationships. Position each unit of text and rectangle in one of the square frames. Once again make yourself aware of the form contrasts and form relationships on pages 74–75.

COMBINING ELEMENTS

Dark planes or columns can be seen as such or as placeholders for pictures, text or headlines. Especially when combining several design elements it can be of great help to initially work with abstract shapes. In this way it is easier to create and control formal relationships and thus easier to keep on top of the material. This also enables you to create several different versions without wasting much time. The work with abstract shapes trains the eye; construction and structure of a design can be recognised more easily and this experience can be integrated into your own work. Arrange several design elements (square, circle, column) in various formats. Set a guide line as axis. Arrange the objects along this axis and thus determine the format's centre of gravity (layout scribble see page 65).

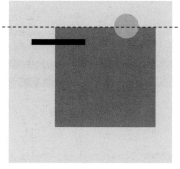

Centre of gravity at the top

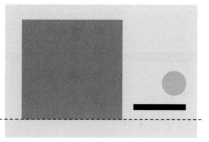

Centre of gravity at the bottom

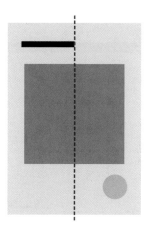

Centre axis

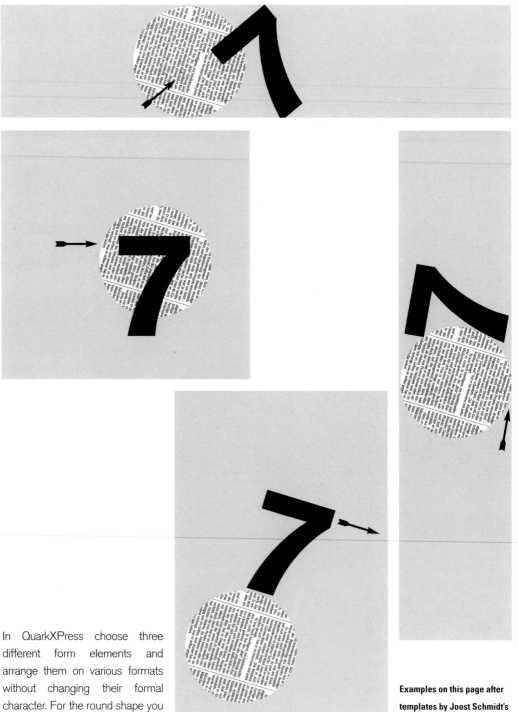

In QuarkXPress choose three different form elements and arrange them on various formats without changing their formal character. For the round shape you can scan a newspaper clipping.

Examples on this page after templates by Joost Schmidt's "Lessons at the Bauhaus".

In Freehand, create various compositions with a square as well as the words "beware wild animals" in a sans-serif font (Helvetica, Arial, Frutiger) on different formats. Find solutions that illustrate the meaning. Use black, white and an accent colour.

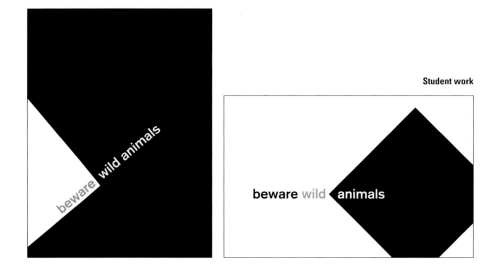

Student work

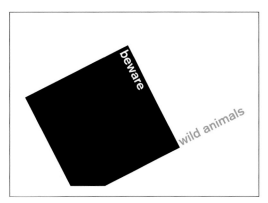

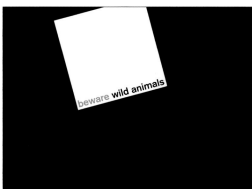

COMPRESSION

The addition of progressively or numerically growing elements is a form of compression. Overlaying individual elements creates a new contour, a new shape develops up to the point where the whole background is "filled". Try this yourself. In the first of nine basic planes on an A4 page position a black square and to each of the following planes add another black square until the background is completely filled (see also page 19).

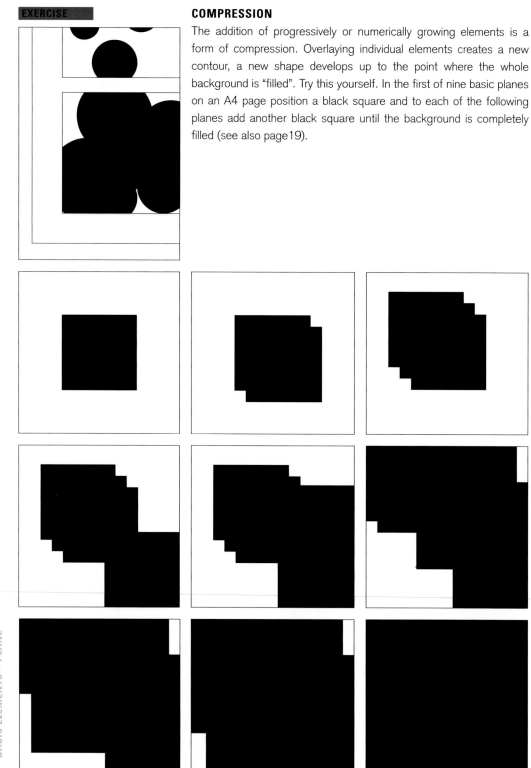

ANALYSIS OF MOTIF AND PLANE

With this exercise you gain more confidence with the division of the plane, the judging of figure to background and form to format relationship. Examine simple illustrations for distinct shapes. Is there a centre of gravity, a stabilising axis? Well-designed postcards or illustrations from magazines can be used as templates. Choose an image that clearly shows a shape, a distinct motif. You can do this exercise on the computer by scanning the image and cutting out the shape in Photoshop. Use the command "Image →" Extract..." or "Select → Colour Range...". Replace motif and background with white or black respectively (see also the exercise on page 132).

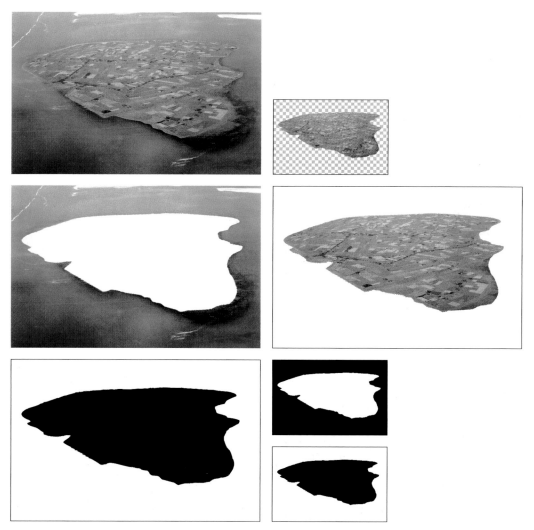

DEALING WITH SHAPES

1 In 6–8 square planes draw with a pencil a form development of a geometrical shape, e.g. a circle to a simple object, like a spoon. **2** In the second part of the exercise use the drawing tool in Freehand: also in 6–8 steps, try, by using black shapes growing into a square, to create an object within this square plane. Approach from two sides – top and bottom or left and right. The shapes grow and, progressing towards the inside, develop the contour of the object. Eventually the background is black and the contour of the figure (object) is white. **3** Arrange the results symmetrically on a new A4 page by duplicating and horizontally flipping them. Observe the newly created form relationships.

"The white surface of paper (despite the present and visible texture) we consider 'empty', an inactive plane. With the first appearance of a dot, a line, the empty plane is activated. A quantity of the plane – albeit small – is thus covered. With this process emptiness becomes white, becomes light; a contrast with the black appearance develops. Light is only visible in relation to shadow. The actual process with drawing and writing is basically not to add black, but to take away light. The essence of the sculptor's work also consists mainly of taking away from the block of stone and in so doing giving it a form; the final shape is what is 'left over' of the material. Looking at a symbol from this angle, it takes on a whole new meaning concerning its ability to communicate. All subsequent thoughts are supported by the duality of 'light and shade', 'white and black'." (Frutiger)

© Student work by
Elmar Kaiser

RULES OF PERCEPTION

Knowing about the structuring of human perception is the basis for every designer. The underlying question is how we psychologically structure and sort optical impulses, combine them and interpret them as formal structures. The "psychology of form", a scientific branch that emerged at the turn of the century, summarised the results of research into visual perception in a large number of "rules of form", of which only the most important ones are explained below. Unlike other laws, the laws of form are not binding rules and principles written in stone, but rather a generally valid synthesis resulting from scientific research and experience.

Rule of Proximity

Identical elements that are close together are combined to create one unity. In this way, several lines of text are perceived as a text block and the gaps and spaces take on a separating role. A word space separates the "unity" of a word in a similar fashion – only then is it possible to perceive individual words as units.

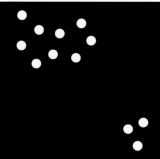

Rule of Closeness

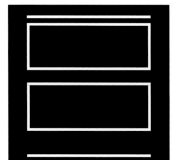

Lines that enclose a plane are more likely to be perceived as a unit than if they aren't closed (see above).

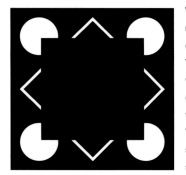

We fill in the missing parts to create familiar forms. The black in the white circles seems darker than in the white corners. Thus we see two superimposed squares.

Rule of Equality

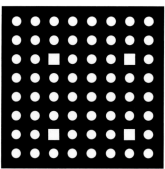

Elements of identical form are combined to create one unity. Here the four little squares form one big square.

Elements of equal size are combined to create one unity. Here the number 5 is made up of 13 larger dots.

Elements of equal brightness are combined to create one unity.

Parallelism is an ordering element. At the same time, parallelism dominates the background: the curvy lines always stay in the foreground.

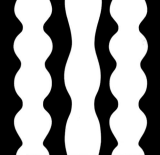

Symmetry leads to closeness. Symmetrical contours are perceived as a figure.

Symmetry leads to closeness. Thus individual parts are not perceived as such.

Rule of the Continuous Line

With overlapping forms, the parts that form familiar shapes through continuous lines are more likely to be perceived as a unity. Thus, in this example we see two circles, rather than two halfmoons facing each other (illustration right). If the overlap is very large or too small, it becomes harder to differentiate (illustration below). With overlapping forms, "correct" differentiation is made possible by this phenomenon of perception.

Trend for Spatiality

Familiar shapes can also be three-dimensional and thus cause a preferred spatial interpretation of an actually two-dimensional representation.

Rule of Experience

We can add the missing parts of a figure from experience. Because we (in Western-European culture) know the latin alphabet, we easily combine the three angles to form an "E". Similarly we use our spatial experience when interpreting illuminated shapes: light coming from the top left makes the shape look convex, coming from the bottom right it makes the shape look concave. Sunlight (from above) and the reading direction play a role. There are nevertheless situations where an unambiguous interpretation is not possible. The last illustration is a detail from the picture "Concave and Convex" by Dutch artist M. C. Escher, who consciously plays with such phenomena of perception.

Tendency to equalise

From a variety of shapes that are based on the same "construction plan", we do not perceive individual forms but instead tend to differentiate only about seven different shapes, i.e. merge them into groups even though they in fact (mathematically) comprise of endless different variants. Hence, if aiming for recognisability, greater numbers of similar elements should not be in groups larger than seven.

Figure-Ground-Relation

No figure exists alone, but in an environment. This can be a background, e.g. a larger, differently shaded figure, or a basic surface, e.g. a sheet of paper. There is a difference of quality between the figure and its surroundings, i.e. a border or contour, caused by the different consistencies. The stronger the difference of quality and explicit the distinction or contrast, the clearer the figure stands out of its surroundings. Soft focus or similar devices can hinder differentiation.

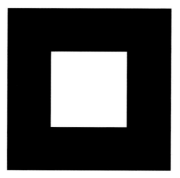

Figure-Ground-Relation and the Rule of Equality

In the illustration top left we see black dots on a white background. If the white square is in turn surrounded by an environment of the same quality as the dots, we combine it to create a whole and see a white perforated shape on a black background.

Figure-Ground-Relation – Inner Side

If a contour doesn't fully enclose a form, the part that is enclosed is recognised as a form. In the first illustration we thus see a white circle on a black background and not a black punched shape on a white background. This becomes even clearer in the second illustration. If the proportions of inner sides are roughly equal, it causes problems with differentiation. Depending on point of view, we see a white shape on a black background or a black shape on a white background.

Figure-Ground-Relation

Only when the line thickness exceeds a certain thickness in relation to the size of the form, we stop seeing it as line, but as an autonomous plane.

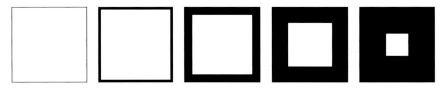

Figure-Ground-Relation and the Rule of Closeness and Equality

The rules of perception also apply to the figure-ground differentiation. Representation of a triangle with minimal means (after Matthaei). In the first row: triangle and white triangle are perceived with imaginary lines. In the second row we see triangles with different contrasts of quality. In the first illustration the contrast of quality is optimal, in the two other illustrations the "Rule of Equality" applies: equal elements are perceived as a closed unity. In the third row the triangles are only visible by their outlines. In the third illustration, watch the different effect of brightness of the three sides: the left side offers most space for hatch lines – that is where the strongest contrast in brightness occurs.

In the abstraction of figures it is for instance possible to show only contour (outlines) and leave out any representation of brightness or colour. We still see the figure with its surface and structure, and not a line as such. The role of the line is merely and solely to enclose a plane or surface in order to present the form. The line by itself has no function.

Figure-Ground-Relation – Differentiation

If the differentiation of figure and ground is more difficult, we initially look for:

– closed planes

– smaller planes

– symmetrical contours or planes

– simpler or more familiar forms

– planes with structures or textures.

Even though our perception organises what we see in such a way that figure and ground are distinguished clearly, there are cases where this isn't easily possible. A classic example is "Rubin's Vase", where one can equally see a vase and two faces.

Figure-Ground-Relation – Environment

To simplify differentiation, the surroundings or background can be enlarged. If for instance the background is white, the smaller black vase is more likely to be perceived as the shape. If in turn the background is black, the white faces are more likely to be perceived as shape. In both cases the larger plane appears as background.

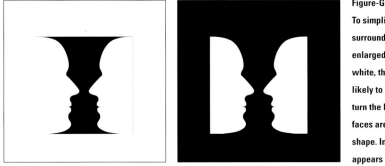

Figure-Ground-Relation – Inner Structuring

Another possibility of clear distinction of figure and background is the application of structure and texture, the so-called inner structuring of form. The structure doesn't necessarily have to emphasise the meaning of the figure. Inner structuring is an important way of separating figures from the background.

1

1 Walter Zeischegg, "Stripe Grid, to clarify
shape and transitions, projected on to
undulating corrugated squares", 1972.
(Printed by kind permission of Rosalinde
Zeischegg.)
2 Andrea Zaumseil, "Untitled", 1999,
pastel on cardboard. (Printed by kind
permission of the artist.)
3 Laurie Anderson, "September 20,
New York Times, Horizontal / China Times,
Vertical", 1971 – 79. (Printed by kind
permission of the artist.)

2

There are a large number of options available when working with brightness, texture or structure. Walter Zeischegg makes space tangible by projecting a striped grid on to a domed surface of his own design. In two dimensions, a comparable effect can be achieved by using correspondingly curved lines. The powerful plasticity and the aesthetic charm of Andrea Zaumseil's work is achieved by smearing chalk marks across rough-textured paper. Laurie Anderson takes the front pages of two newspapers – one each from the Eastern and Western hemispheres – and "weaves" them into an indecipherable "information texture".

BRIGHTNESS – TONE VALUE

So far, we have been working mainly with black and white, in order to study the effects of various compositional elements: form, size, position, quantity, proportion and rhythm. Brightness is one more method of differentiation, and thus constitutes a further compositional tool. To be precise, brightness is a partial aspect of colour. Yet the achromatic colours – black, white and the various shades of grey – play a very special role in design. Areas of varying brightness "distance themselves" from one another, create contrast, and produce three-dimensional effects. Brightness is a material quality. It is a product of the concentration (or superimposition) of other compositional elements on the original surface. In printing technology, for example, the various shades of grey are produced by (grid-) dots and lines of different magnitudes or densities. By enlarging or multiplying single elements, one can reduce the proportion of white in the surface area – the surface becomes darker.

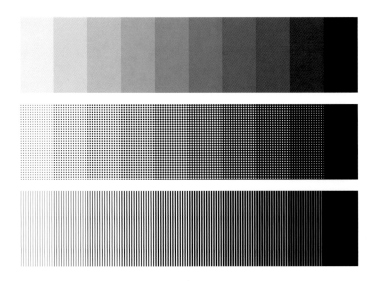

EXERCISE In QuarkXPress, create planes of varying tone value by **1** using equally distanced lines of differing thickness and by **2** using lines of the same thickness with differing distances. Sort by tone value.

hardly perceivable
plane shape

plane shape is
perceivable

clear plane shape

plane shape
interacting with
background

Only by its lightness a plane distinguishes itself from its surroundings and is perceived as such. An interaction of plane and background happens if two planes of widely differing tonal values meet — depending also on size and position of the plane in relation to the background.

Simultaneous contrast happens when two or more planes of differing lightness or colour interact. It applies to the actual planes (plane contrast) as well as their edges (edge contrast).

Although the objective lightness of the little squares is identical, the impression of lightness changes with the surroundings: The darker the background, the lighter the squares seem to be.

The objective lightness of the circles is the same. Again the impression of brightness changes with the differing size of the plane in relation to its background: The larger the dark part and smaller the light part, the brighter the light element seems to be.

Adjacent to a dark plane, the edge of a light plane seems brighter than the rest of the light plane — conversely the edge of the dark plane seems darker than the rest of the dark plane.

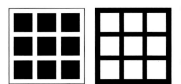

Together, plane and edge contrasts also cause the perception of equally sized planes as smaller or larger depending on their brightness.

BRIGHTNESS – TONE VALUE – SPATIALITY

The linear superimposition of form suffices to produce a perspectival space (above left). When this superimposition is combined with the use of graduated grey values from black to light grey (the tonal values are given as percentages; here, 20%, 40%, 70% and 100%), the result is an impression of abstract spatial depth, as shown in the illustration (below left). Depending on where the black surface is located, it is either pushed forward or compacted. "Between black and white lies an infinite graduation of grey tones, which form the path that leads the eye from light into darkness."

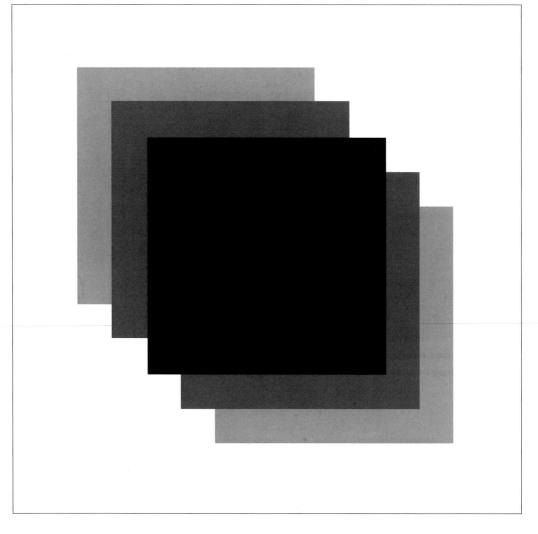

Use nine different plane compositions from the exercise on page 72 and save them EXERCISE with a new name. Change the brightness to a selection of five different greys. Create compositions that sequentially vary the different shades of grey.

In the second part of the exercise, create another nine plane compositions but this time EXERCISE with three different shades, consisting of a selection of squares of two different sizes. Try to make use of the spatial effect of the shades of grey.

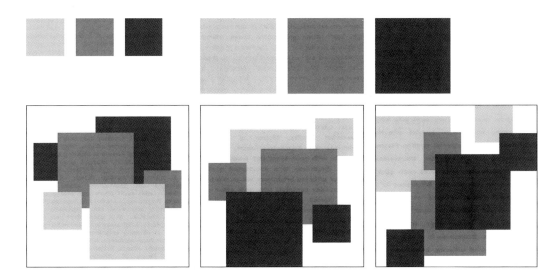

type style:	type style:	type style:
thin (regular)	thin (regular)	thin (regular)
type size: 5 pt	type size: 5 pt	type size: 5 pt
leading: 10 pt	leading: 8 pt	leading: 6 pt
kerning: 5	kerning: 0	kerning: - 5

type style:	type style:	type style:
medium (demi-bold)	medium (demi-bold)	medium (demi-bold)
type size: 5 pt	type size: 5 pt	type size: 5 pt
leading: 10 pt	leading: 8 pt	leading: 6 pt
kerning: 5	kerning: 0	kerning: - 5

type style:	type style:	type style:
bold	bold	bold
type size: 5 pt	type size: 5 pt	type size: 5 pt
leading: 10 pt	leading: 8 pt	leading: 6 pt
kerning: 5	kerning: 0	kerning: - 5

FONT AND GREYS

Text blocks form grey values. The grey value of a text can be influenced by the size, face and kerning of the font, as well as by the leading. When designing text for reading, the goal should be consistent, uniform brightness – but the line spacing must also be generous enough to allow easy legibility. By means of differentiated grey values, pages can be better structured and more interestingly organised, and important passages of text can be given added emphasis.

Planes of differing brightness set themselves apart, produce contrasts with each other and create spatial effects. Brightness is a substantial quality. Planes of differing brightness set themselves apart, produce contrasts with each other and create spatial effects. Brightness is a substantial quality. Planes of differing brightness set themselves apart, produce contrasts with each other and create spatial effects. Brightness is a substantial quality. Planes of differing brightness set themselves apart, produce contrasts with each other and create spatial effects. Brightness is a substantial quality. Planes of differing brightness set themselves apart, produce contrasts with each other

Planes of differing brightness set themselves apart, produce contrasts with each other and create spatial effects. Brightness is a substantial quality. Planes of differing brightness set themselves apart, produce contrasts with each other and create spatial effects. Brightness is a substantial quality. Planes of differing brightness set themselves apart, produce contrasts with each other and create spatial effects. Brightness is a substantial quality. Planes of differing brightness set themselves apart, produce contrasts with each other and create spatial effects. Brightness is a substantial quality. Planes of differing brightness set themselves apart, produce contrasts with each other and create spatial effects. Brightness is a substantial quality. Planes of differing brightness set themselves apart, produce contrasts with each other and create spatial effects.

Planes of differing brightness set themselves apart, produce contrasts with each other and create spatial effects. Brightness is a substantial quality. Planes of differing brightness set themselves apart, produce contrasts with each other and create spatial effects. Brightness is a substantial quality. Planes of differing brightness set themselves apart, produce contrasts with each other and create spatial effects. Brightness is a substantial quality. Planes of differing brightness set themselves apart, produce contrasts with each other and create spatial effects. Brightness is a substantial quality. Planes of differing brightness set themselves apart, produce contrasts with each other and create spatial effects. Brightness is a substantial quality. Planes of differing brightness set themselves apart, produce contrasts with each other and create spatial

Planes of differing brightness set themselves apart, produce contrasts with each other and create spatial effects. Brightness is a substantial quality. Planes of differing brightness set themselves apart, produce contrasts with each other and create spatial effects. Brightness is a substantial quality. Planes of differing brightness set themselves apart, produce contrasts with each other and create spatial effects. Brightness is a substantial quality. Planes of differing brightness set themselves apart, produce contrasts with each other and create spatial effects. Brightness is a substantial quality. Planes of differing brightness set themselves apart, produce contrasts with each other and create spatial effects. Brightness is a substantial quality. Planes

Planes of differing brightness set themselves apart, produce contrasts with each other and create spatial effects. Brightness is a substantial quality. Planes of differing brightness set themselves apart, produce contrasts with each other and create spatial effects. Brightness is a substantial quality. Planes of differing brightness set themselves apart, produce contrasts with each other and create spatial effects. Brightness is a substantial quality. Planes of differing brightness set themselves apart, produce contrasts with each other and create spatial effects. Brightness is a substantial quality. Planes of differing brightness set themselves apart, produce contrasts

Planes of differing brightness set themselves apart, produce contrasts with each other and create spatial effects. Brightness is a substantial quality. Planes of differing brightness set themselves apart, produce contrasts with each other and create spatial effects. Brightness is a substantial quality. Planes of differing brightness set themselves apart, produce contrasts with each other and create spatial effects. Brightness is a substantial quality. Planes of differing brightness set themselves apart, produce contrasts with each other and create spatial effects. Brightness is a substantial quality. Planes of differing brightness set themselves apart, produce contrasts

Planes of differing brightness set themselves apart, produce contrasts with each other and create spatial effects. Brightness is a substantial quality. Planes of differing brightness set themselves apart, produce contrasts with each other and create spatial effects. Brightness is a substantial quality. Planes of differing brightness set themselves apart, produce contrasts with each other and create spatial effects. Brightness is a substantial quality. Planes of differing brightness set themselves apart, produce contrasts with each other and create spatial effects. Brightness is a substantial quality. Planes of differing brightness set themselves apart, produce contrasts with

Planes of differing brightness set themselves apart, produce contrasts with each other and create spatial effects. Brightness is a substantial quality. Planes of differing brightness set themselves apart, produce contrasts with each other and create spatial effects. Brightness is a substantial quality. Planes of differing brightness set themselves apart, produce contrasts with each other and create spatial effects. Brightness is a substantial quality. Planes of differing brightness set themselves apart, produce contrasts with each other and create spatial effects. Brightness is a substantial quality. Planes of differing brightness set themselves apart, produce contrasts with each other and

Planes of differing brightness set themselves apart, produce contrasts with each other and create spatial effects. Brightness is a substantial quality. Planes of differing brightness set themselves apart, produce contrasts with each other and create spatial effects. Brightness is a substantial quality. Planes of differing brightness set themselves apart, produce contrasts with each other and create spatial effects. Brightness is a substantial quality. Planes of differing brightness set themselves apart, produce contrasts with each other and create spatial effects. Brightness is a substantial quality. Planes of differing brightness set themselves apart, produce contrasts with each

In an A4 document in QuarkXPress create the text blocks shown on the left ("Style → Alignment: Justified") with three different font styles of a Linear-Antiqua Sans-serif font (e.g. Arial or Helvetica). The given specifications are for guidance only and might have to be varied depending on the text used, typeface and type width. Make sure that the text blocks give an even impression of grey, which is where even word spacing comes into effect. You might have to change the "H&Js-settings" in the "Edit menu" or adjust the hyphenation manually (position the cursor in the desired place and press ⌘). To adjust the kerning, select all text (⌘ A) and go to "Style → Kern..." or "Style → Character...". The desired value is entered in

"Kern Amount". In the "H&Js dialog box" you can save these settings or alter them if needed. "Justified text": In justified text the word and character spacing is automatically varied in order to achieve equal length of line within a paragraph. Text with generous leading can take slightly enlarged word spacing. Hence: The optimum word spacing is 100%, the minimum should differ only slightly from this, and the maximum can be enlarged. Altered kerning generally has an adverse effect

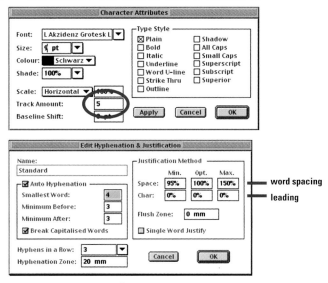

on the look of the body text, which is why the value for minimum, optimum and maximum is 0% and should only be changed with very narrow text columns.

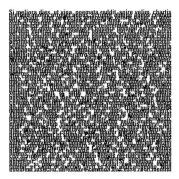

Si meliora dies, ut vina, poemata reddit, scire velim, chartis pretium quotus arroget annus. scriptor abhinc annos centum qui decidit, inter perfectos veteresque referri debet an inter vilis atque novos? Excludat iurgia finis, "Est vetus atque probus, centum qui perficit annos." Quid, qui deperiit minor uno mense vel anno, inter quos referendus erit? Veteresne poetas, an quos et praesens et postera respuat aetas? "Iste quidem veteres inter ponetur honeste, qui vel mense brevi

Extreme settings affect legibility but can be attractive graphical solutions.

GREYS – RHYTHM

1 Type a word repeatedly in a text frame until the frame has been filled completely (for example, in Arial regular, 9 pt). Duplicate the frame six times and distribute the frames evenly on a DIN A4 page. Lay out the word you have chosen rhythmically by changing only **2** the leading, **3** the kerning, **4** the font size, **5** the font size and/or the typeface version. You should also find other solutions than those illustrated here. Then, using the same methods, try to visualise other words.

1
```
wegung, Bewegung, Bewegung, Bewegung, Bewegung, Bewegung, Bewegung
Bewegung, Bewegung, Bewegung, Bewegung, Bewegung, Bewegung, Bewegung
Bewegung, Bewegung, Bewegung, Bewegung, Bewegung, Bewegung, Bewegung
Bewegung, Bewegung, Bewegung, Bewegung, Bewegung, Bewegung, Bewegung
Bewegung, Bewegung, Bewegung, Bewegung, Bewegung, Bewegung, Bewegung
Bewegung, Bewegung, Bewegung, Bewegung, Bewegung, Bewegung, Bewegung
Bewegung, Bewegung, Bewegung, Bewegung, Bewegung, Bewegung, Bewegung
Bewegung, Bewegung, Bewegung, Bewegung, Bewegung, Bewegung, Bewegung
Bewegung, Bewegung, Bewegung, Bewegung, Bewegung, Bewegung, Bewegung
Bewegung, Bewegung, Bewegung, Bewegung, Bewegung, Bewegung, Bewegung
Bewegung, Bewegung, Bewegung, Bewegung, Bewegung, Bewegung, Bewegung
Bewegung, Bewegung, Bewegung, Bewegung, Bewegung, Bewegung, Bewegung
Bewegung, Bewegung, Bewegung, Bewegung, Bewegung, Bewegung, Bewegung
Bewegung, Bewegung, Bewegung, Bewegung, Bewegung, Bewegung, Bewegung
Bewegung, Bewegung, Bewegung, Bewegung, Bewegung, Bewegung, Bewegung
Bewegung, Bewegung, Bewegung, Bewegung, Bewegung, Bewegung, Bewegung
Bewegung, Bewegung, Bewegung, Bewegung, Bewegung, Bewegung, Bewegung
Bewegung, Bewegung, Bewegung, Bewegung, Bewegung, Bewegung, Bewegung
Bewegung, Bewegung, Bewegung, Bewegung, Bewegung, Bewegung, Bewegung
Bewegung, Bewegung, Bewegung, Bewegung, Bewegung, Bewegung, Bewegung
Bewegung, Bewegung, Bewegung, Bewegung, Bewegung, Bewegung, Bewegung
Bewegung, Bewegung, Bewegung, Bewegung, Bewegung, Bewegung, Bewegung
Bewegung, Bewegung, Bewegung, Bewegung, Bewegung, Bewegung, Bewegung
Bewegung, Bewegung, Bewegung, Bewegung, Bewegung, Bewegung, Bewegung
```

2
```
wegung Bewegung Bewegung Bewegung Bewegung Bewegung Bewegung
Bewegung Bewegung Bewegung Bewegung Bewegung Bewegung Bewegung
Bewegung Bewegung Bewegung Bewegung Bewegung Bewegung Bewegung
Bewegung Bewegung Bewegung Bewegung Bewegung Bewegung Bewegung
Bewegung Bewegung Bewegung Bewegung Bewegung Bewegung Bewegung
Bewegung Bewegung Bewegung Bewegung Bewegung Bewegung Bewegung
Bewegung Bewegung Bewegung Bewegung Bewegung Bewegung Bewegung
Bewegung Bewegung Bewegung Bewegung Bewegung Bewegung Bewegung
Bewegung Bewegung Bewegung Bewegung Bewegung Bewegung Bewegung
Bewegung Bewegung Bewegung Bewegung Bewegung Bewegung Bewegung
Bewegung Bewegung Bewegung Bewegung Bewegung Bewegung Bewegung
Bewegung Bewegung Bewegung Bewegung Bewegung Bewegung Bewegung
Bewegung Bewegung Bewegung Bewegung Bewegung Bewegung Bewegung
Bewegung Bewegung Bewegung Bewegung Bewegung Bewegung Bewegung
Bewegung Bewegung Bewegung Bewegung Bewegung Bewegung Bewegung
Bewegung Bewegung Bewegung Bewegung Bewegung Bewegung Bewegung
Bewegung Bewegung Bewegung Bewegung Bewegung Bewegung Bewegung
Bewegung Bewegung Bewegung Bewegung Bewegung Bewegung Bewegung
Bewegung Bewegung Bewegung Bewegung Bewegung Bewegung Bewegung
Bewegung Bewegung Bewegung Bewegung Bewegung Bewegung Bewegung
```

2
```
wegung, Bewegung, Bewegung, Bewegung, Bewegung, Bewegung
Bewegung, Bewegung, Bewegung, Bewegung, Bewegung, Bewegung
Bewegung, Bewegung, Bewegung, Bewegung, Bewegung, Bewegung
Bewegung, Bewegung, Bewegung, Bewegung, Bewegung, Bewegung
Bewegung, Bewegung, Bewegung, Bewegung, Bewegung, Bewegung
Bewegung, Bewegung, Bewegung, Bewegung, Bewegung, Bewegung
Bewegung, Bewegung, Bewegung, Bewegung, Bewegung, Bewegung
Bewegung, Bewegung, Bewegung, Bewegung, Bewegung, Bewegung
Bewegung, Bewegung, Bewegung, Bewegung, Bewegung, Bewegung
Bewegung, Bewegung, Bewegung, Bewegung, Bewegung, Bewegung
Bewegung, Bewegung, Bewegung, Bewegung, Bewegung, Bewegung
Bewegung, Bewegung, Bewegung, Bewegung, Bewegung, Bewegung
Bewegung, Bewegung, Bewegung, Bewegung, Bewegung, Bewegung
Bewegung, Bewegung, Bewegung, Bewegung, Bewegung, Bewegung
Bewegung, Bewegung, Bewegung, Bewegung, Bewegung, Bewegung
Bewegung, Bewegung, Bewegung, Bewegung, Bewegung, Bewegung
Bewegung, Bewegung, Bewegung, Bewegung, Bewegung, Bewegung
Bewegung, Bewegung, Bewegung, Bewegung, Bewegung, Bewegung
Bewegung, Bewegung, Bewegung, Bewegung, Bewegung, Bewegung
Bewegung, Bewegung, Bewegung, Bewegung, Bewegung, Bewegung
```

2
```
Bewegung, Bewegung, Bewegung, Bewegung, Bewegung, Bewegung,
Bewegung, Bewegung, Bewegung, Bewegung, Bewegung, Bewegung,
Bewegung, Bewegung, Bewegung, Bewegung, Bewegung, Bewegung,
Bewegung, Bewegung, Bewegung, Bewegung, Bewegung, Bewegung,
Bewegung, Bewegung, Bewegung, Bewegung, Bewegung, Bewegung,
Bewegung, Bewegung, Bewegung, Bewegung, Bewegung, Bewegung,
Bewegung, Bewegung, Bewegung, Bewegung, Bewegung, Bewegung,
Bewegung, Bewegung, Bewegung, Bewegung, Bewegung, Bewegung,
Bewegung, Bewegung, Bewegung, Bewegung, Bewegung, Bewegung,
Bewegung, Bewegung, Bewegung, Bewegung, Bewegung, Bewegung,
Bewegung, Bewegung, Bewegung, Bewegung, Bewegung, Bewegung,
Bewegung, Bewegung, Bewegung, Bewegung, Bewegung, Bewegung,
Bewegung, Bewegung, Bewegung, Bewegung, Bewegung, Bewegung,
Bewegung, Bewegung, Bewegung, Bewegung, Bewegung, Bewegung,
Bewegung, Bewegung, Bewegung, Bewegung, Bewegung, Bewegung,
Bewegung, Bewegung, Bewegung, Bewegung, Bewegung, Bewegung,
```

2

Bewegung, Bewegung, Bewegung, Bewegung, Bewegung, Bewegung, Bewegung, ... (repeated typographic pattern)

3

Bewegung, Bewegung, Bewegung, Bewegung, Bewegung, Bewegung,
Bewegung, Bewegung, Bewegung, Bewegung, Bewegung, Bewegung,
Bewegung, Bewegung, Bewegung, Bewegung, Bewegung, Bewegung,
Bewegung, Bewegung, Bewegung, Bewegung, Bewegung, Bewegung,
Bewegung, Bewegung, Bewegung, Bewegung, Bewegung, Bewegung,
Bewegung, Bewegung, Bewegung, Bewegung, Bewegung, Bewegung,
Bewegung, Bewegung, Bewegung, Bewegung, Bewegung, Bewegung,
Bewegung, Bewegung, Bewegung, Bewegung, Bewegung, Bewegung,
Bewegung, Bewegung, Bewegung, Bewegung, Bewegung, Bewegung,
Bewegung, Bewegung, Bewegung, Bewegung, Bewegung, Bewegung,
Bewegung, Bewegung, Bewegung, Bewegung, Bewegung, Bewegung,
Bewegung, Bewegung, Bewegung, Bewegung, Bewegung, Bewegung,
Bewegung, Bewegung, Bewegung, Bewegung, Bewegung, Bewegung,
Bewegung, Bewegung, Bewegung, Bewegung, Bewegung, Bewegung,
Bewegung, Bewegung, Bewegung, Bewegung, Bewegung, Bewegung,
Bewegung, Bewegung, Bewegung, Bewegung, Bewegung, Bewegung,
Bewegung, Bewegung, Bewegung, Bewegung, Bewegung, Bewegung,
Bewegung, Bewegung, Bewegung, Bewegung, Bewegung, Bewegung,
Bewegung, Bewegung, Bewegung, Bewegung, Bewegung, Bewegung,
Bewegung, Bewegung, Bewegung, Bewegung, Bewegung, Bewegung,
Bewegung, Bewegung, Bewegung, Bewegung, Bewegung, Bewegung,
Bewegung, Bewegung, Bewegung, Bewegung, Bewegung, Bewegung,
Bewegung, Bewegung, Bewegung, Bewegung, Bewegung, Bewegung,
Bewegung, Bewegung, Bewegung, Bewegung, Bewegung, Bewegung,
Bewegung, Bewegung, Bewegung, Bewegung, Bewegung, Bewegung,
Bewegung, Bewegung, Bewegung, Bewegung, Bewegung, Bewegung,

4

Bewegung, Bewegung, Bewegung, Bewegung, Bewegung,
Bewegung, **Bewegung**, Bewegung, Bewegung, Bewegung,
Bewegung, Bewegung, **Bewegung,** Bewegung,
Bewegung,
Bewegung, Bewegung, Bewegung, Bewegung,
Bewegung,
Bewegung,
Bewegung, Bewegung,
Bewegung, Bewegung, Bewegung, Bewegung,
Bewegung, Bewegung, Bewegung, Bewegung,
Bewegung, Bewegung, Bewegung, **Bewegung**
Bewegung,
Bewegung, Bewegung, Bewegung, Bewegung, Bewegung,
Bewegung, Bewegung, Bewegung, **Bewegung**, Bewegung,
Bewegung, Bewegung, Bewegung, Bewegung, Bewegung,
Bewegung, Bewegung, Bewegung, **Bewegung,**
Bewegung, Bewegung, Bewegung, **Bewegung,**
Bewegung
Bewegung, Bewegung, Bewegung, Bewegung, Bewegung,
Bewegung, Bewegung, Bewegung, Bewegung, Bewegung,
Bewegung, Bewegung, Bewegung, Bewegung, **Bewegung,**

5

Bewegung

VARIETY OF GREYS

Brightness, tonal values or shades of grey can be derived from an achromatic scale ranging from black to white. At the same time, brightness is a partial aspect of colour, for each colour has its own specific brightness. You can confirm this by printing a coloured design on a black-and-white printer: a yellow area will appear considerably lighter than a violet one, for example. In addition, each particular colour can also appear in various different degrees of brightness. Pure black, white and grey are achromatic. The gradations of brightness – the grey tones – are, however, only seldom truly achromatic; often, they will display the tiniest nuances of chromatic colour. This is what makes grey tones so incredibly varied. One way of making grey tones is by mixing a colour with black or white; but they can also be produced by mixing approximately equal parts of the primary colours or by mixing complementary colours (see the chapter entitled "Colour"). In this way, increasing fuzziness in coloured images leads to a mixing of the colours and thus, ultimately, to grey. A neutral grey is a grey without any detectable hue. The eye can perceive even the smallest shifts in the proportions, and is thus capable of registering hues (including unwelcome ones). Grey tones are particularly strongly affected by simultaneous contrast (see pages 138 and 159).

A neutral grey can consist of a tonal step on the scale of black and white.

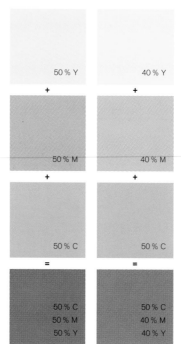

50 % Y	40 % Y
+	+
50 % M	40 % M
+	+
50 % C	50 % C
=	=
50 % C	50 % C	30 % C
50 % M	40 % M	25 % M
50 % Y	40 % Y	25 % Y
		35 % K

A neutral grey can also consist of the three primary colours cyan, magenta and yellow (body colours; print colours). In the CMYK-mode you cannot achieve a neutral grey by mixing equal parts of the three colours. To achieve this equal percentages of magenta and yellow and a slightly higher percentage of cyan must be mixed. A grey of exactly equal parts of the three colours seems brownish. In the printing process, black is often added as the grey stabiliser, to avoid tinting.

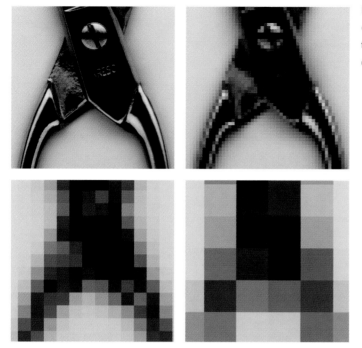

If you split a seemingly grey image (CMYK or RGB) in Photoshop into cells with the filter "Pixelate → Mosaic...", you can discover the great variety of greys.

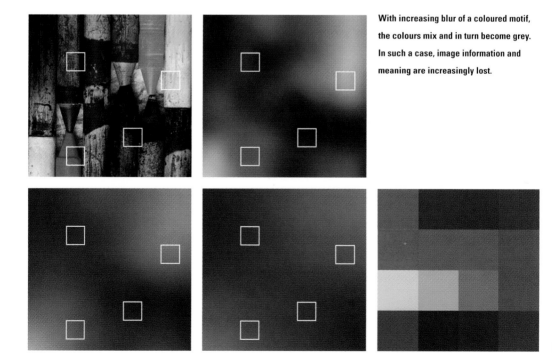

With increasing blur of a coloured motif, the colours mix and in turn become grey. In such a case, image information and meaning are increasingly lost.

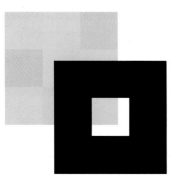

Try and identify these individual greys. All are part of the grey modulation below. You can also use a small passe-partout (see page 11) in order to view the tones individually.

Modulation rows are created through step-by-step grades from a colour to grey, white or black. These are modulation scales of grey (also see next page).

30 % C 11 % M 23 % Y					20 % C 13 % M 13 % Y
18 % C 11 % M 23 % Y					20 % C 13 % M 13 % Y
18 % C 23 % M 23 % Y					20 % C 13 % M 13 % Y
18 % C 23 % M 11 % Y					20 % C 13 % M 13 % Y
30 % C 23 % M 11 % Y					20 % C 13 % M 13 % Y
30 % C 11 % M 11 % Y					20 % C 13 % M 13 % Y

Produce a series of modulations of grey using Freehand. **1** Create a square element. **2** Clone it once and move it horizontally. **3** In a colour mode (e.g. CMYK), mix the base colour (for example, blue) as well as the final colour in the modulation series (grey). **4** Fill each element respectively with one colour. Select both elements. **5** Now select the command "Blend" from the "Xtras-function" ("Xtras → Create → Blend"). **6** In the object panel, under "Steps", set the desired number of intermediary stages (confirm by pressing the command key). **7** If you wish to specify the precise composition of the newly-created colours, then you must ungroup the group that has arisen as a result of blending (⌘ ⇧ G). **8** Now select the command "Xtras → Colours → Name All Colours". All colours will appear in the colour panel. Proceed in the same way with all subsequent colours. To achieve harmonious modulations, you must enter the same number of "steps" for each new colour.

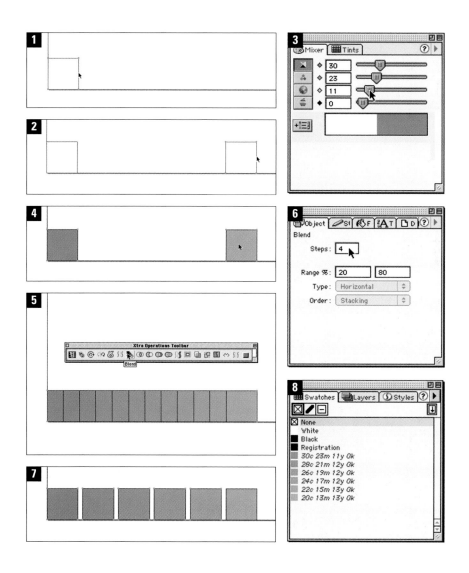

Colours of a modulation row to grey, white or black always appear harmonious, no matter which order or selection of colour.

Base colour = 100 %
secondary colour
(of varying mix)

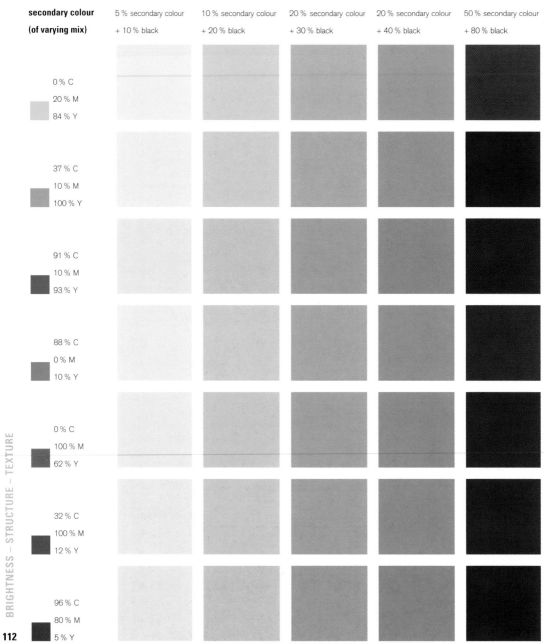

	5 % secondary colour + 10 % black	10 % secondary colour + 20 % black	20 % secondary colour + 30 % black	20 % secondary colour + 40 % black	50 % secondary colour + 80 % black
0 % C 20 % M 84 % Y					
37 % C 10 % M 100 % Y					
91 % C 10 % M 93 % Y					
88 % C 0 % M 10 % Y					
0 % C 100 % M 62 % Y					
32 % C 100 % M 12 % Y					
96 % C 80 % M 5 % Y					

Freehand offers even more ways of producing modulations. **1a** A modulation to white can be produced with the "Colour Mixer" panel ("Windows → Panels → Colour Mixer"). To do so, drag a defined colour from the Colour List Panel on to the colour field on the left of the "Colour Mixer" panel (if necessary, first enter the command "Xtras → Colours → Name All Colours"). Select the desired shade by clicking on it or entering it. **1b** A modulation to black can be achieved by dragging a defined colour (including any colour that has already been modulated to white) to the left colour field of the "Colour Mixer" panel. Turn the black modulator up until you reach the desired percentage figure (here, 40%). **2** The completed hue can now either be dragged back into the "Colour List" panel or directly on to the object that is to be filled. Now produce modulations like those illustrated, or find modulations of your own.

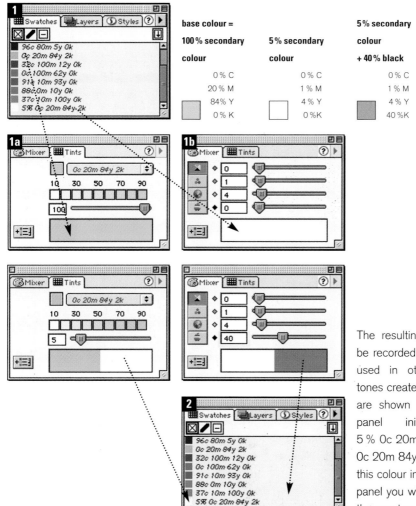

base colour =

100 % secondary colour

	0 % C
	20 % M
	84% Y
	0 % K

5 % secondary colour

	0 % C
	1 % M
	4 % Y
	0 %K

5% secondary colour + 40 % black

	0 % C
	1 % M
	4 % Y
	40 %K

The resulting colour values can be recorded and in this way also used in other programs. The tones created in the "Tints Panel" are shown in the "Colour List" panel initially like this: 5 % 0c 20m 84y 0k, (i.e. 5 % of 0c 20m 84y 0k). If you now drag this colour into the "Colour Mixer" panel you will be able to read off the exact cmyk-percentage.

SPATIALITY – VOLUME – PERSPECTIVE

Graphic design is basically restricted to two dimensions. Spatiality, volume and perspective can only be simulated. The simplest way of doing so, as you have seen already, is to superimpose various layers of areas with graded tonal values. Another option is to use "large" and "small" to indicate proximity and distance, the impression of perspective being produced by imaginary connecting vanishing lines. In a purely linear representation, a strong illusion of spatiality can be achieved by choosing certain visual angles (see the illustration top right). If this is done clearly enough, a two-dimensional representation can give a three-dimensional impression – the illusion of volume. This spatial effect can be increased by using differentiated tonal values. Drop shadows can further increase the illusion of three-dimensional space. Rather than continuing on the topic of perspectival constructions, however, we shall now show how linear representations can be augmented by the various compositional ways of indicating volume.

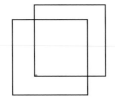

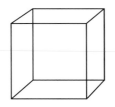

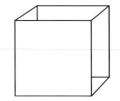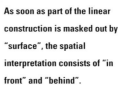

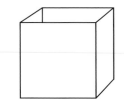

This initially is a linear construction: two overlapping squares. With merely this simple overlay a spatial impression is very vague.

Now the two squares are connected by diagonal guides which allows for a spatial interpretation – a cube is created.

As soon as part of the linear construction is masked out by "surface", the spatial interpretation consists of "in front" and "behind".

With two sides of the cube as opaque surfaces, the image of a volume is very definite.

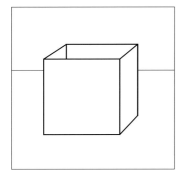

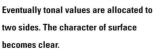

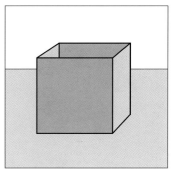

Here the three-dimensional drawing of an open cubical box on a square plane is shown with a horizon line. The horizon line shows the perspective of the object in a spatial context.

Eventually tonal values are allocated to two sides. The character of surface becomes clear.

Now all sides as well as the floor on which the object is positioned have been allocated tonal values that hint at the direction of light and the shaded side.

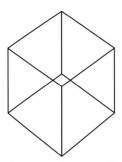

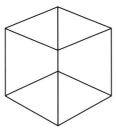

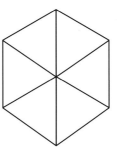

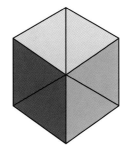

A natural, random perspective is advantageous for spatial interpretation. Here a three-dimensional object is recognisable.

Here it is already harder to recognise an object as two vertical edges merge into one.

Here a spatial interpretation is unlikely as all edges meet in one point. More likely it is perceived as a two-dimensional "symbol".

Only a differentiation through different shades allows for a clearer definition.

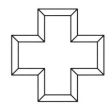

If these insights are applied to a symbol, it becomes evident that with an exactly symmetrical vanishing point the volume is not ideally represented – especially in the lower half.

In this example the vanishing point was chosen randomly so that all building lines are visible which clearly shows the volume. At the same time, the low perspective shows the position of the viewer.

A similar situation as the previous one: here also the volume is clearly visible, but this time the position of the viewer is elevated.

A spatial impression is created through seemingly sloping edges but it isn't clear whether the structure is raised or depressed (also see page 94).

LIGHT AND SHADE

Plasticity, then, can also be represented in two dimensions by using different tonal values or progressions of tonal values. This is one way of simulating how light is cast – and where there is light, we also find shade. Besides its own tonal value, an object has a light side and a side in shade – and it also casts its own shadow on its surroundings. The illuminated side is lighter, while the shaded side is normally in darkness. The location of the shade indicates the direction from which the (invisible) light is arriving. Since most people are right-handers, a light source located above left is presumed optimal, for the writing or drawing hand will then cast no shadow on the image area. The illustration on the left shows several circles in relief. Use these to test which direction the shadow should be in if the representation of a cylinder is to "feel right". Experience shows that most people will choose the first example illustrated, in which the shadow falls on the lower right. The reverse example, with the shadow on the upper left, is generally perceived as a round hole with its upper wall in the shade. In photos of inscriptions or reliefs, for example, the direction from which the light falls determines how we perceive them: as reliefs (raised) or as engravings (depressed) (see also page 94). By projecting a drop shadow on to an imaginary background, it is also possible to make a symbol or a figure stand out from the background. (Acknowledgements to Frutiger.)

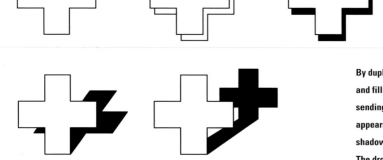

By duplicating the cross, moving the copy and filling it in with black, as well as sending it to the back, the white cross appears lifted from the floor, casting a shadow on to an imaginary background. The drop shadow can also be projected on to an imaginary floor (and wall) in which case the shadow itself takes on a perspective shape.

UNUSUAL VOLUMES AND TROMPE-L'OEIL

Designers can use unusual perspectives or consciously employ impossible perspectives in order to disorientate the observer (see illustrations in the top row below).

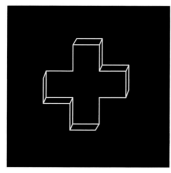 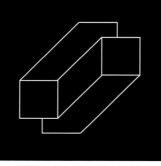 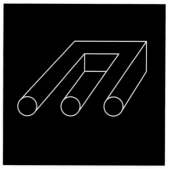

For the work of a designer, it is important to know about the differences between a perceived and an actual state of affairs (e.g. between the perceived and the measured length of an object) – the so-called optical illusions or trompe-l'oeils. A representation which is "exact" in a geometrical-mathematical sense may nonetheless "look wrong". In such cases, it must be replaced by a "right" representation. And of course, the optical-illusion phenomena can also be used deliberately to strengthen the effect and the importance of particular compositional elements. Trompe-l'oeils normally result from a combination of exact figures with representations that suggest volume or direction. This is what produces the discrepancy in the observer's awareness, the disparity between what is rationally known and what is visually perceived.

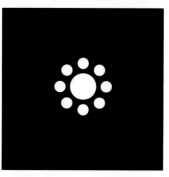

The right judgement of size also depends on the surroundings. The inner circles of the two flowers are identically sized (illustrations on right), but the circle in the small flower seems bigger. The contrast between big and small affects the judgement of size.

On perspectively progressing lines equally sized elements appear larger "towards the back" as "in front" (illustration below). The person in front appears a dwarf, the one in the middle normal-sized and the one in the back a giant. The square is distorted into a trapezium (below right).

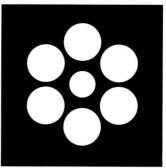

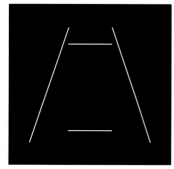  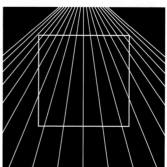

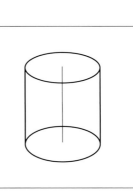

Round objects can be created with the help of tonal blends.

Another method of lending objects plasticity is to work with progressions from light to dark. The impression of corporeality is produced by the simulated fall of light. Here too, this impression is manifested in varying tonal values. The object's appearance alters according to the location of the imagined light source. There are however, strict limitations on the extent to which DTP programs can produce realistic, plastic representations of three-dimensional objects. Much better and more detailed images can be generated in 3D programs such as "3D-Studio-Max" for Windows or "Electric Image" for Mac. By means of the "rendering" process, a feature of these programs, surface structures and textures (as well as lighting effects) can be applied to objects. In the next section of this chapter, we shall turn our attention to structures and textures of a two-dimensional nature.

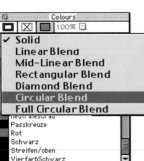

Gradation tools in QuarkXPress, Freehand and Photoshop. Freehand and Photoshop offer better possibilities for the creation of gradations as the direction of light can be determined.

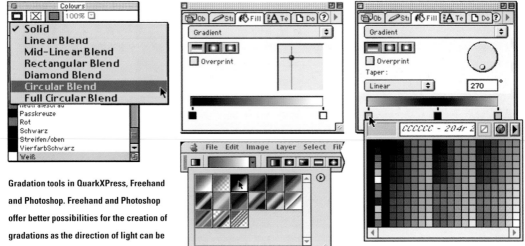

Fill simple geometrical shapes with various tonal gradations. Arrange
the shapes alongside or overlapping each other.

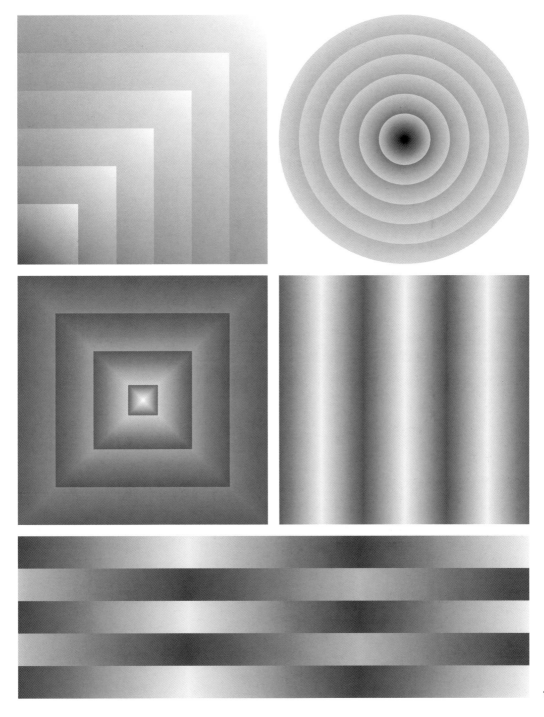

LINES – TONE VALUES – SPATIALITY

Two-dimensional structures can also be generated through the thickening of lines. Depending on the strength and density of the lines, different tonal values can be achieved, which in turn enable the production of spatial effects.

1 Create various spatial forms in Freehand or QuarkXPress by shifting lines of equal length equidistantly. **2** In Freehand, using "Windows → Panels → Xtras" (see page 111 for detailed instructions), create tangible shapes from two differently-sized, parallel, linear forms. Utilise a variety of line widths and a varying number of in-between steps.

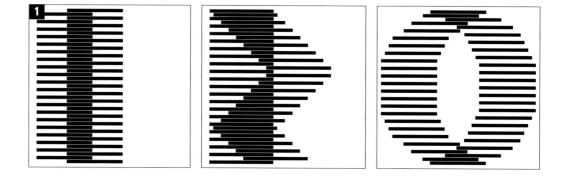

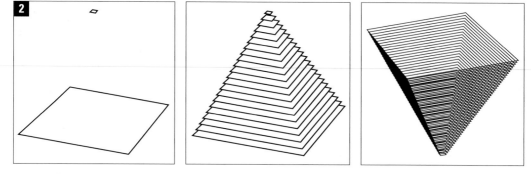

1 In Freehand, create a narrow rectangle (2 x 66 mm length), fill it in with black. Clone the strip (⌘ ⇧ D), move it by 2 mm ("Transform-Panel") and fill it in with white. **2** Select both strips, clone and move again (by 4 mm), until the plane is filled (10 times). Open a circle (without fill) and position as shown. Select all strips and copy into the clipboard (⌘ C). **3** Now click on the circle and apply the command "Edit → Paste Inside". **4** Rotate the circle by −9° ("Transform Panel"). **5** Set the stroke of the circle to "none". Clone the circle another time, rotate again by −9° and reduce the size to 90%. **6** Repeat the last action a few times. Experiment in the other exercises with different shapes and transformations.

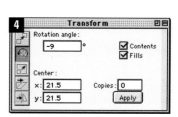

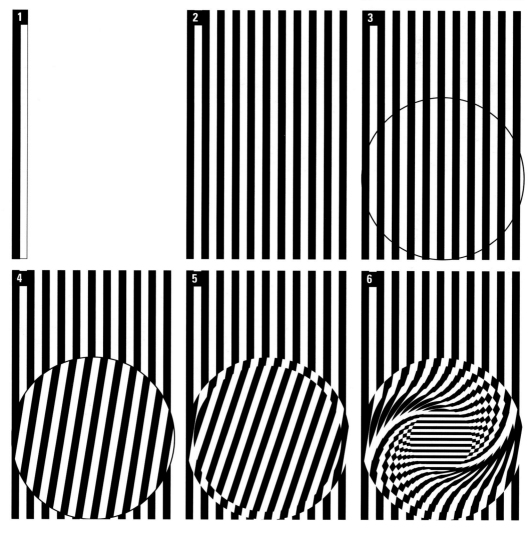

FROM BRIGHTNESS TO STRUCTURE

It is only a small step from brightness to structure (and texture). To be exact, brightness is expressed in structure. The screen representation of every image containing tonal values consists of pixels of varying brightness – in other words, we are dealing with a pixel structure. If the image is printed out, the tonal values are converted into a halftone pattern – or rather, a dot structure. The purpose of the following exercise is to make visible a small number of technical structures that are seldom noticed. In QuarkXPress, load a "TIF" image which you have saved in Photoshop under "Mode: Greyscale". Duplicate the image several times. Activate the Content Tool and select an image. Experiment with the "Contrast" and "Halftone" settings found in the Style menu. Keep in mind: the halftone settings cannot be seen on the screen; they only become visible on the print-out from a postscript capable printer (or a printer with a software RIP).

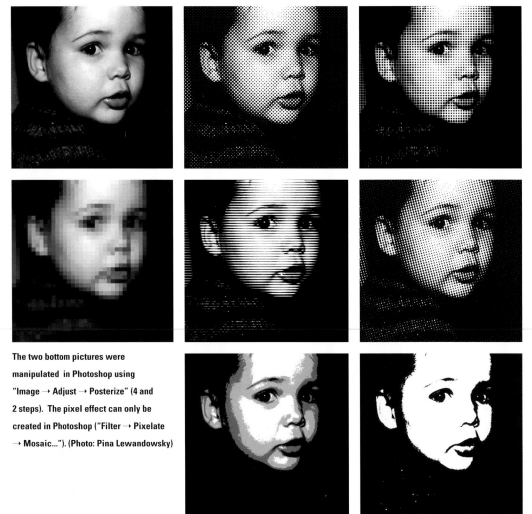

The two bottom pictures were manipulated in Photoshop using "Image → Adjust → Posterize" (4 and 2 steps). The pixel effect can only be created in Photoshop ("Filter → Pixelate → Mosaic..."). (Photo: Pina Lewandowsky)

It is advisable to draw structures by hand at least once as well. Put a piece of transparent paper over a photo, tape both down and copy the image's contours with a black fine drawing pen. Put another piece of transparent paper on top of the first and then fill in the individual areas with different structures. It is important here to pay attention to how the structures separate optically, or, in other words, which structures come forward and which remain in the background. Your sketches should utilise hatching, dotted areas or other similar techniques. Experiment with the effects of simple structures.

© **Student work by Constanze Kebernik, Aasia Malik, Elmar Kaiser**

SYSTEMATIC APPROACH TO STRUCTURES AND TEXTURES

In principle, one differentiates between "structures" and "textures". Structures are flat in nature and usually registered optically. Textures are surface characteristics created by the quality of the material, and are primarily registered haptically (through the sense of touch). In two-dimensional form, the boundaries can often be unclear since, in the end, the original texture becomes a (flat) area through scanning or any other process of reproduction. Now find some photo examples, load the scans into the image window and arrange them into groups according to structure or texture.

STRUCTURES

plane structures

(registered optically)

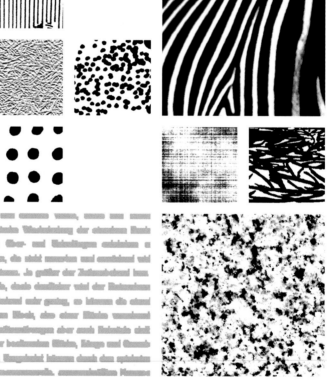

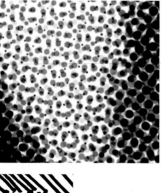

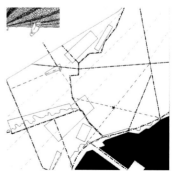

TEXTURES

tangible structures

(registered haptically)

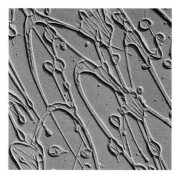

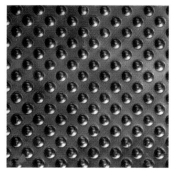

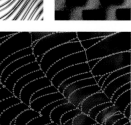

TACTILE TABLE*

The "Tactile Table" is a collection of materials with surface structures; or, to be more exact, fabric materials categorised by characteristics (structures) and perceptions (effects). Link the adjectives listed here

ATTRIBUTES (CONSISTENCIES)

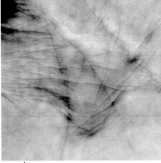
organic

smooth, metallic

crumbly

stable, firm

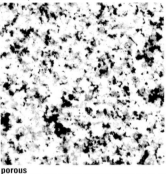
porous

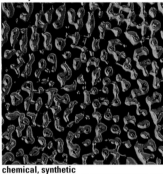
chemical, synthetic

artificial

intricate

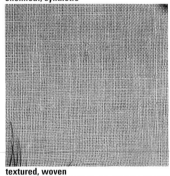
textured, woven

cracked

stony

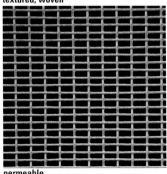
permeable

BRIGHTNESS – STRUCTURE – TEXTURE

126

to the image details (scans). Think of other adjectives and sort them by characteristics and perceptions as well, or find surface structures to which you yourself can assign characteristics or perceptions.

* The expression "Tactile Table" was coined by Maholy-Nagy, an artist who was also active at the "Bauhaus".

SENSATIONS (IMPRESSIONS)

rough, dry

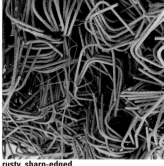

rusty, sharp-edged

matt, water-resistant

soft

prickly, scratchy

wet

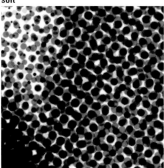

documentary

supple, flowing

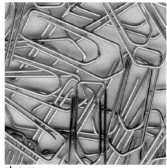

obscure

architectural, constructive

moving, restless

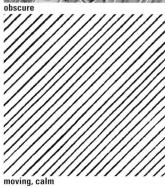

moving, calm

DISCOVERING STRUCTURES

In Photoshop, open one each of the surface structures (scans) you have found. Add a new layer on top of this, and fill it in with white. Reduce the opacity of this layer (e.g. to 50%), so that you can see

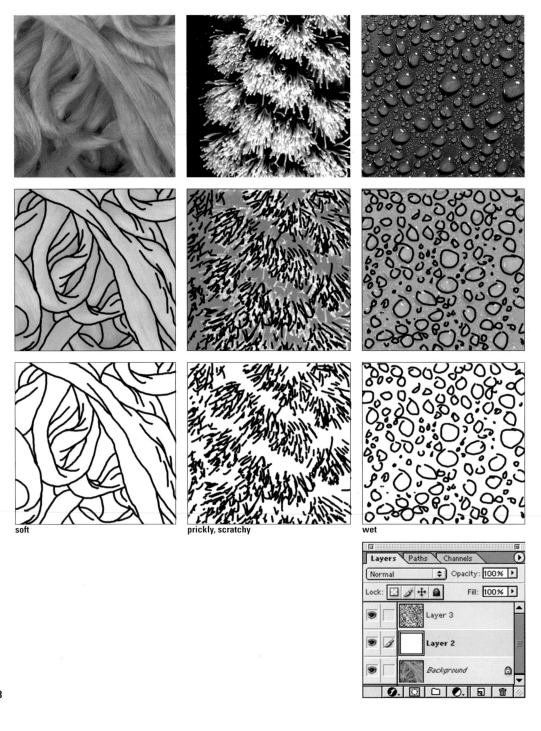

soft

prickly, scratchy

wet

the background through it. Now take another new layer and copy some of the most striking characteristics of the structure. You should appropriate tools for this (a paintbrush, for example), and a graphics tablet is helpful, but not necessary. The point is not to make a detailed and faithful copy, but to grasp the essential nature of the structure in question. When you have finished, restore the opacity of the white-filled surface to 100%, restore the document to one level and save it for your materials collection under a new name.

The structures shown here have all been created in Photoshop with the Pencil Tool or the Paintbrush.

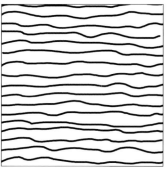

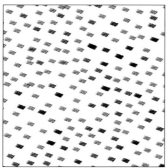

Investigate the design possibilities of Photoshop by means of one or more (two-dimensional) structures. Your aim should be to preserve the flat quality by making minimal alterations to the structure. Open a structure file in Photoshop. If possible, choose a square image format. Duplicate the structure layer. **1** Select a square surface and apply transformations or a filter to it (e.g. "Filter → Other → Minimum…"). If you are satisfied with the result, duplicate the structure level and experiment with other filters. Save each of the results separately as a TIF. In QuarkXPress, create one or more DIN A4 pages containing these structures. Arrange the results according to formal criteria, such as fragmentation or changes in size or direction.

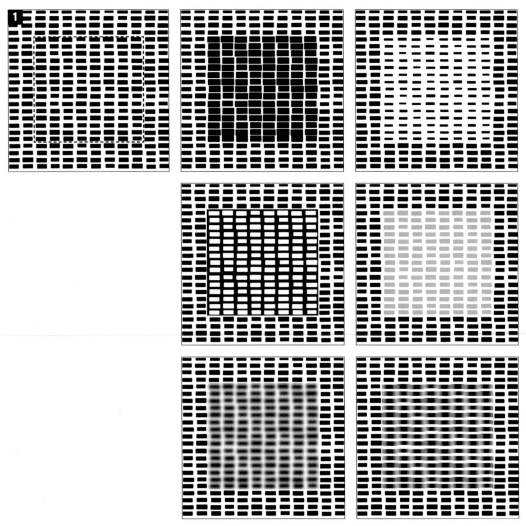

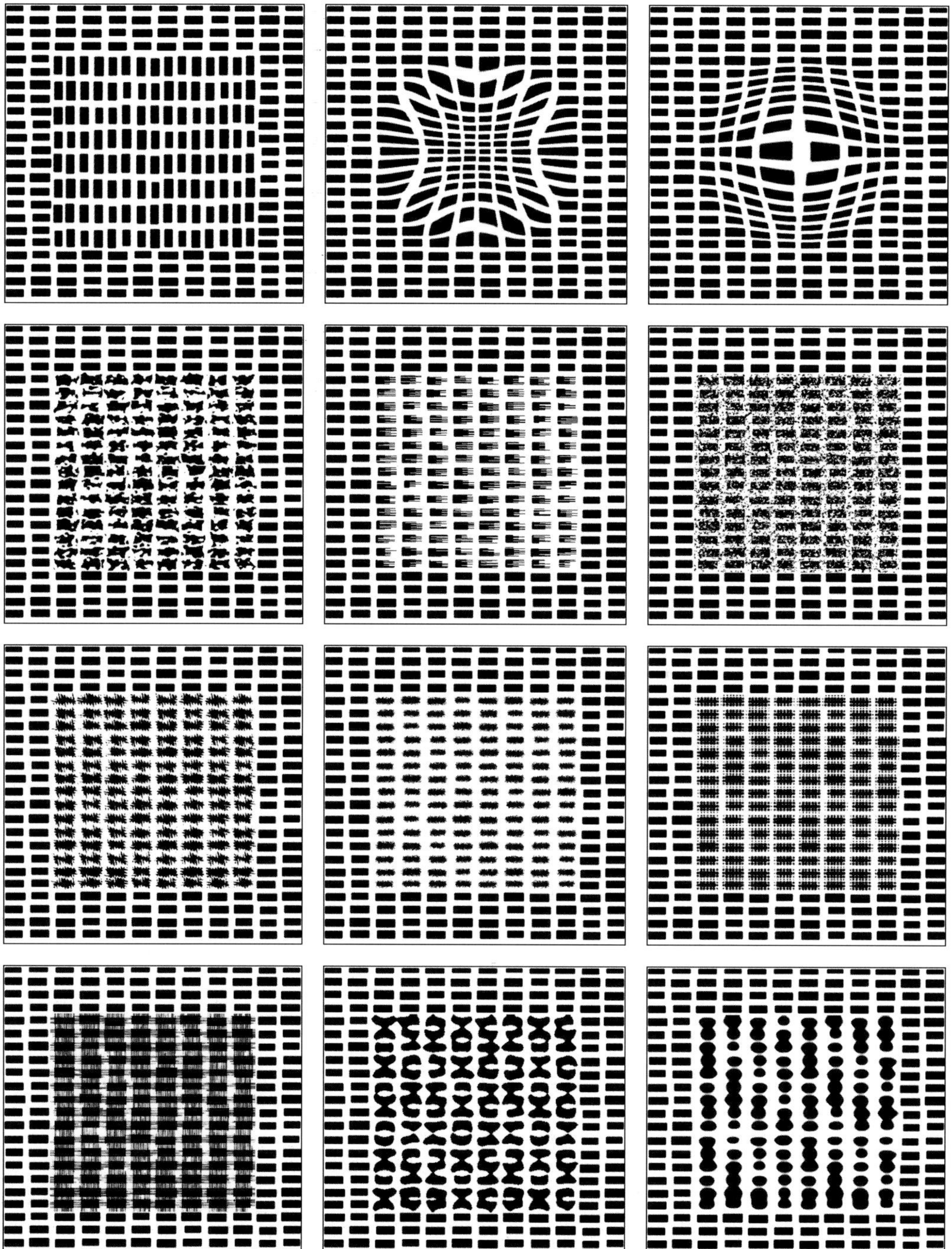

ANALYSIS OF MOTIF, PLANE AND STRUCTURE

In the chapter "Analysis of motif and plane" (see page 89), we already separated motif from surface. Utilising the same procedure, image content can be filled in with grey tones and/or structures. In doing this, the effects of structure depiction can be easily examined; for example, which structures contrast more strongly and separate themselves more, or which combinations come across more flatly or create a spatial effect. As described previously, select a picture which contains a clear-cut figure or a definite motif. Scan in the picture and open Photoshop. Select the appropriate motif and replace the image and background with other structures or textures. Alter the contents by using "foreign" structures, too.

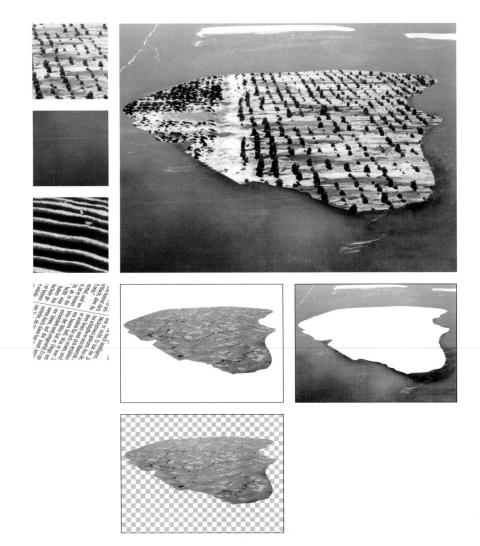

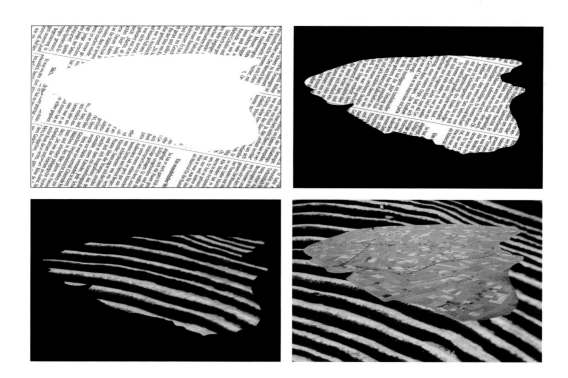

1

2

3

"Portraits"

1 Rupprecht Geiger, "101, '780/87'", 1987, acrylic on canvas 285 x 170 cm. (Printed by kind permission of the artist. Photo: Philipp Schönborn.)

2 Josef Albers, "Homage to the Square", 1964, oil on masonite, 121 x 121 cm (© ProLitteris, 2002, 8033 Zürich).

3 Josef Albers, "Homage to the Square", 1950, tempered ardor, 45 x 45 cm (© ProLitteris, 2002, 8033 Zürich).

4 Imi Knoebel, "Portraits", 1991, acrylic on wood, 50 x 35 cm. (Printed by kind permission of the artist.)

Colour contrast, colour spatial appearance and colour effects are the realm of the so-called minimalists. Rupprecht Geiger also experimented with colour spatial impacts. He particularly likes to work with minimal contrast and a swatch of saturated reds.

The simple compositions of squares by Josef Albers facilitate undisturbed perception of differing, adjacent colours.

Imi Knoebel's portraits express moods of colour and are therefore inspiring for the exercises with colour in this chapter.

NO COLOUR WITHOUT LIGHT

In space complete darkness prevails. For millions of years the sun has produced electromagnetic waves which are emitted uniformly into space in all directions. Lightness only comes from the sun's rays falling on objects, including particles, which occur in the earth's atmosphere. Only a small proportion of the rays are visible to the naked eye, and it is this which is characterised as "light". The other wave frequencies of the sun's rays, such as ultraviolet or infrared rays, affect us in unseen ways. We define a neutral light – that is white light – as daylight. Of course this neutral daylight consists of several wave frequencies. The physicist Isaac Newton in the 17th century was the first to render the different frequencies visible through a glass prism. He saw the light emanating from the prism as a continuous line of colours, the so-called spectral band, and distinguished red, orange, yellow, green, blue, indigo and violet. A refraction of light, such as that taking place through a prism, can be observed in the rainbow or quite simply with a CD. The exact frequencies of visible light were determined later by the physicist Thomas Young; they lie between 400 and 700 nm. The percentage distribution of the colours may fluctuate sharply according to the type of light. This is the reason why now and again coloured objects appear to reflect very different colours in different lights. Looking at such a spectral band it is possible to see that red, green and violet (today we say blue) are represented much more strongly than the other colours. It has been recognised that all other colours can be blended from these three colours of white light (red, green and blue) by projecting them on top of each other and therefore white light can be produced again. Thus these three colours are termed primary colours (primary = original). White comes into being in this way through the greater lightness of all three primary colours – whilst by contrast black through the fact that no light is present. The mixing principle for light colours is termed additive as all emitted frequencies (emission) are completely returned (remission).

The colour theory Goethe espoused was (apparently) different and he tried, completely unsuccessfully, to refute Newton. According to Goethe, colours originated from grey, the so-called murky colour on the light-dark borders, through the changing effect of light and darkness. In support of this Goethe quoted, amongst other examples, that of observation of nature, where bright sunlight is colourless and only appears red for example in the dismal evening twilight. He observed white strips of paper on a black background through test tubes and discovered so-called border spectres, predominantly in the colours yellow, blue and purple. In his theory Goethe also confirmed the gyration test, where Newton arranged his seven basic colours on a circle according to their spectral percentages: on rotation (i.e. optical mixing), grey appeared instead of the expected white. Goethe did this by designing a chromatic circle with yellow, blue and purple as primary colours; it received less support from physicists than from artists and pointed the way to the colours used today in printing technology. Goethe's model is one of the body colours (not a counterpart to the light colours), which are produced when light falls on objects, and which because of their surface spectral properties swallow (absorb) certain light frequencies, only returning a part. This is why the mixing principle of body colours is called subtractive. These primary colours are nowadays identified as cyan, magenta and yellow. All other colours can be mixed from them, through overlayering and altering their intensity. This is very evident in ink-jet printing and colour

700 nm

600 nm

500 nm

400 nm

copying, which use these exact colours. However, here black must be inserted as the fourth colour because in practice it is not possible to produce a deep black with just the three primary colours. Practically all colours that are not light colours are counted as body colours, for example mark colours, printing ink and enamel paint. Here are two theories that do not in fact contradict the present state of knowledge: the physicist looks into a matter from a scientific perspective, the artist relies on what he sees with his own eyes. Today we know the principle behind the light colours (white light consists of the basic colours red, green and violet, i.e. blue) and behind the body colours (when light falls on a pigment, because of its spectral properties, it absorbs its complementary colour and reflects its own colour).

An important tip: because of the different properties inherent in light and body colours, it is not possible to portray light colours with body colours – as for example by printing the entire colour spectrum of light colours. Conversely on a screen that works with light colours body colours can only be simulated. This caveat must therefore be applied to all the colours and definitions used here. A complementary contrast between, for example,

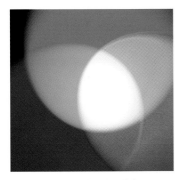

Light colours: All colours result from overlapping projection of particular wave ranges of visible light. The primary colours (red, green, blue) together make up white.

Body colours: Certain spectral ranges of light are absorbed when illuminating body colours. All colours are a product of intensity changes and overlapping. The primary colours (cyan, magenta, yellow) together make up black.

Body colours: Four-colour (offset) print works with the same principle. The change of intensity is achieved through rasterising and the tones of colours through overprint of the primary colours. The actual mixing is done by the eye.

red and green has impact and force both on the screen and in the printing ink. A grey-tone selected on the monitor will, when printed, never look like it does when portrayed on the screen. Pure colours for printing must therefore be mixed in CMYK mode and, if standard colours are not being used, it is necessary to preselect colours from a colour pattern book (e.g. Euroskala). These colours cannot be judged from a monitor!

COLOUR PHYSIOLOGY: IMPRESSION AND PERCEPTION

Viewed physically, our world is colourless. The impression of colour in our brain is only created through the effect of light on the one hand and on the other the human reaction to this purely physical attraction and its reception via the eyes. Physiology is, in general, the theory of the foundations of human life. A subsidiary field, sense physiology, has been researching for many years now the effects of the physical attraction of light on our organism. Research into the eye has shown that, for different types of reception, there exist on the retina two types of sense cells, equal but different in shape. The cones take over sight during the day and also the recognition of colours, the rods take over in reduced light, when only sensations of lightness are evoked. (At night all cats are grey.) Although explicit functions are ascribed to these two cell types, they interact to deliver different sense impressions.

A vivid example is the effect of grey on different coloured backgrounds. Although the colour grey is clearly defined here, it will be experienced differently in different surroundings. There is, as yet, no general theoretical explanation for this physiological problem – it is not an optical illusion. As designers we must however take these factors into account and deploy them purposefully. For now let us briefly return to the colour impressions that precede the perception of colour. Colour impressions can be very polymorphic (the explanations and examples on the page on the right are based on the subtractive system).

In colour perception, various physiological phenomena can be observed. We perceive an objectively identical colour differently depending on its surroundings ("simultaneous contrast"). With coloured backgrounds the perception of colour changes – similarly a mid-grey seems darker on a white than on a black background.

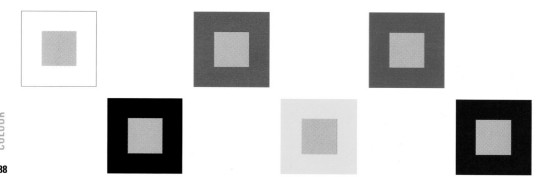

Light or dark: light colours are mostly called pastel colours, i.e. colours that have been lightened by adding white. In contrast, dark colours are composed with black, or simply darker.

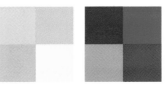

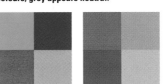

Bright or tinted: The primary colours of the additive and subtractive colour system are perceived as bright colours. Black and white stand in greatest contrast to bright colours, grey appears neutral.

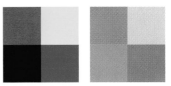

Saturated or desaturated: Saturated colours are full, "untinted" colours, mostly secondary colours, i.e. the colours between primary colours. Desaturated colours are colours mixed with black, white or grey.

Shiny or matt (not illustrated here): Shiny colours are metallic colours (pigments of finest metal) like silver tones, gold etc. It is not possible to illustrate "shiny" colours here – they are printed with metallic ink as special finishes and are available from specialised manufacturers.

Clear or clouded: Clear bright colours appear luminous. They are not achievable in a normal 4-colour offset print process that was used to print this book. These colours are special colours available e.g. from the PANTONE system. Cloudy or tinted colours, so-called tertiary colours contain percentages of all three primary colours of the subtractive colour spectrum. According to the primary colours, these are olive, ochre, umbra, bordeaux, aubergine and petrol tones.

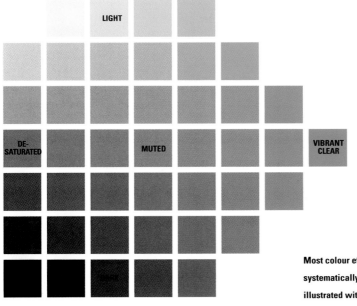

Most colour effects can be represented systematically – in this example illustrated with green tones.

COLOUR PHYSIOLOGY: ASSOCIATION AND EFFECT

Colour psychology is concerned with experiencing colour, the link with archetypical images, possible associations, as well as effects, impressions and emotions. Archetypical images come from the so-called collective unconscious (the philosopher C. G. Jung coined the concept). These are the experiences and associations which people (from a particular culture group) apparently have in common, without consciously reflecting on them. For example the following criteria of archetypes are applied to the six elementary colours (cited by Gerritsen):

Red: the blazing force of fire, symbol of war, blood and violence, symbolic force for the ego; green: the elemental force of fertility which allows the scattered seeds to germinate, symbol of peace and well-being, symbolic colour of rest; blue: the colour for the power of infinity, the sky and the whole firmament, of thought and meditation, symbolic colour of space and eternity; yellow: the force of the natural order of time, sun, moon and stars, symbol of the power of God, symbolic colour of radiance, time and the transience of time; black: the oppressive power of darkness, symbol of death and transience, symbol of grief; white: the dazzling light of the spirit, triumphing over death, the white ash when fire is extinguished, the stillness of the snow that has covered the winter wood, symbol of purity, of the unsullied.

Many different associations can arise from colour impressions while archetypical images merge in with them. Turtschi, who even distinguishes the six elementary colours according to positive and negative attributes, is quoted by way of example here:

Yellow – positive: Colour of beginnings, new, colour which is there before the activity begins; strategy; law; serenity; knowledge; transparency, inspiration, enlightenment; to see through, understand, recognise from plans, creative searching, rational; objective; exhiliration; friendly; lightness of heart; archaic smile. Yellow – negative: Conceit, pretension, arrogance, insolence; emotional superficiality. Orange – positive: Effectiveness; efficiency; economic principle; management; a mix of yellow (strategy/law) and red (action). Orange – negative: Coarseness; churlishness, loutish; technocratic; insensitive. Red – positive: Embodiment of gaiety; vitality, kinetic energy; extreme dynamism and passion; activation; excitement; exertion; the most exquisite pleasures; short duration; creative powers; the will to achieve something; power; not thinking much – doing; personal; individual; maximum joie de vivre. Red – negative: Chaos, violence; repression, the form of crowds. Magenta – positive: Changing one's ways; self-examination; religious colour; revise one's thinking; reflect; colour of repentance and purification; combination of red (power/action) and blue (preservation/conservation) reveals dignity; antithesis of yellow: deviation from rules and regulations gives way to play; ornamentation; irrational; arabesques; superfluous; mysterious, mysticism; vague. Magenta – negative: Naïvety, unworldliness. Blue – positive: Colour of results; outcome; colour of resolution; expanding into the infinite; distance; cooling after heat; nirvana; relaxation; regeneration; shared experience; emotional exchange; chill; consolidation; building of structure; crystalisation; preservation; loyalty; custom; tradition; letting go; contented. Blue – negative: Rigidity; satiety; hyperconservative. Green – positive: Neutral colour on the axis; peace; impersonal; representative; integrated; regenerating; restorative;

colour of fertility; brings new life; objective; retains the overall picture; unemotional.
Green – negative: indecisiveness; cannot define; does not want to commit; laziness.

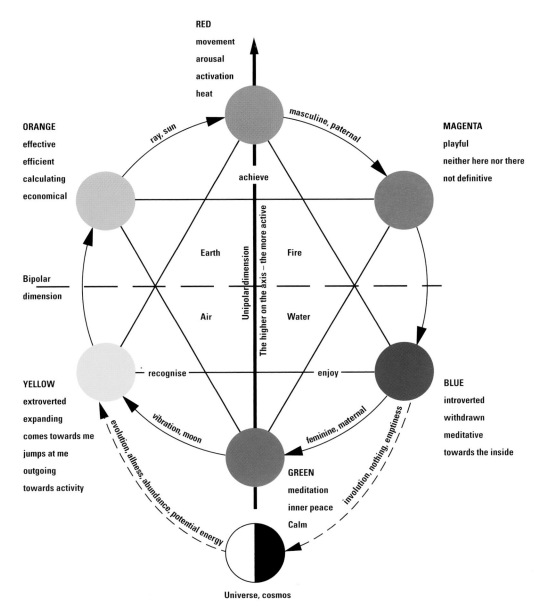

COLOUR ASSOCIATIONS

Colour associations are the contents of consciousness stimulated through colour impressions. When one sees the colour red, one does not only see the colour itself, but links the impression of colour intellectually to experiences and observations. Usually these associations are suffused with archetypes. Thus one might register tomato, fire, blood, Coca-Cola, a Stop sign, lipstick or love. Put together a chart of one or more primary colours as depicted on the facing page. You can cut out pictures you have found or sections of pictures – if this is possible – and paste or otherwise scan them and arrange them into an A4 document in QuarkXPress. You will establish that this exercise is not exclusively concerned with colour and associations but at the same time with material qualities, thus a relation to structures and textures can be established (see page 126).

Mood or sense associations of six elementary colours (according to Küthe / Venn), in which moods and senses can be stimulated:

	mood-specific associations	sense-specific associations
red	active, stimulating, challenging bossy, cheerful	hot, loud, full, strong, sweet, firm
orange	hearty, luminous, lively happy, carefree	warm, saturated, close, glowing, dry, crumbly
yellow	light, clear, free, moved	very light, smooth, sour
green	calming, relaxed, pieceful budding, refreshing, passive	juicy, moist, sour, poisonous young, full
blue	assured, peaceful, distanced, far	cool, wet, smooth, quiet, strong, big
violet	dignified, gloomy, dubious, unhappy	minor sound, rotten sweet, narcotic scent

Possible contrasts with mood- and sense-specific associations can be:

calming – activating	static – dynamic
masculine – feminine	spartan – extravagant
simple – luxurious	formal – playful
cosy – technical	cool – warm
functional – romantic	carefree – sincere

Within the effects of contrasts, associations can be differentiated and emphasised.

However, associations also appeal to our capacity for experience and mental ability. Experiences are always connected with factual knowledge (positive and negative). Both hopes and fears can be triggered by colours and colour combinations. Mental ability (intellectual achievement) means that certain associations are triggered by colour combinations, through which wider-ranging interpretations can materialise.

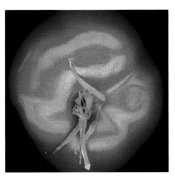

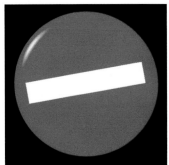

Create twelve picture frames in a new A4 document in QuarkXPress. Attach one of the concepts suggested here to each frame and add a caption underneath it. Fill each picture frame intuitively with a suitable colour (Edit → Colours...). Let other experimentees carry out the exercise and compare the results. Do you agree? Discuss the different choices.

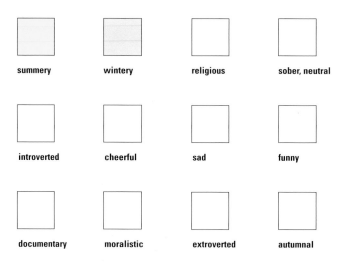

summery	wintery	religious	sober, neutral
introverted	cheerful	sad	funny
documentary	moralistic	extroverted	autumnal

When you have worked with colours for longer you will be able to discover your own colour palettes. This time find colour combinations from four colours for the same concepts as in the previous exercise. Then try the same exercise later with nine colour fields. You will establish that the associations increase when more colours are added.

introverted

cheerful

summery

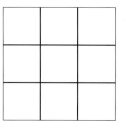

In QuarkXPress, reproduce the colour planes presented here in a new A4 document (mix the colours as they appear to the eye, the differences between print and screen representation have to be ignored in this exercise). Relate the colours to the listed concepts and place them centrally above the respective colour field.

Envy
Fear
Respect
Tolerance
Violence
Steal
Courage
Honour
Pride
Victim
Strangers
Friends

Associations may be heightened considerably through the use of colour combinations. Convert moods (e.g. exciting, calming, light, gloomy) or sensations (e.g. warm, cool, fresh, stagnating) into colour collages. For this exercise it is recommended that you work by hand without a computer as this way it is easier to work spontaneously and intuitively. Cut or tear out sections of a picture and coloured paper. Move each snippet within a frame (print-out of an A4 page with six square frames) until you are satisfied with the result and then paste it in. Label the frames. You can use the following chart (cf. Heller) as a stimulus or comparison, but try to find differing solutions.

MOOD	BASE COLOURS	ACCENT COLOURS
Pleasurable	Green, Pink	Blue, White, Orange, Yellow
Calming	Green, Blue	Pink, White
Simple	White	Red, Green, Blue
Elegant	Black, White, Silver	Violet, Grey, Blue
Friendly	Blue, Pink, Yellow, White	All warm colours
Functional	White, Grey	Black, Blue, Silver
Comfortable	Blue, Beige, Pink	Green, Yellow, Blue
Technical	Silver, Grey	Magenta, Violet, Yellow
Youthful	Green, Pink, Yellow	Blue, White
Cheerful	Red, Yellow, Orange	Green, Blue, Pink
Neutral	White, Grey	–
Luxurious	Gold, Yellow, Violet	Silver, Black, Red
Funny	Red, Orange, Yellow	Pink, White, Blue
Extravagant	Purple, Violet	Gold, Silver, Black
Masculine	Blue, Black	Brown, Red, Silver
Feminine	Pink, Red, White	Blue, Orange, Yellow
Romantic	Pink, White	Green, Orange
Original	Violet, Orange, Silver	All accent colours
Fantastic	Violet, Blue, Yellow	All vibrant colours
Splendiferous	Gold, Red, Magenta	Violet, Grey
Formal	White, Grey, Blue	Black, Silver
Tender	Pink, Blue, White	All warm colours
Pure	White, Blue	–
Spartan	White	–
Silence	Green, White, Blue	Grey, Black, Silver
Warm	Red, Orange, Brown	Yellow, Gold
Activating	Red, Orange, Yellow	Grey, Blue
Dynamic	Red, Blue	Orange, Silver, Yellow
Cool	Blue, Silver, White	Grey
Traditional	Beige, Brown, Gold	Green, Orange

With colour combinations associations can be heightened (colour associations cf. Heller).

Repelling

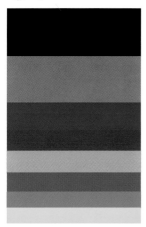

Aggression

Activity

Old

Old-fashioned

Blatancy

Pleasant

Adapted

Aromatic

THE JOHANNES ITTEN COLOUR STAR

Many natural laws of creative colour theory can be studied from a chromatic circle or colour star. Itten's colour star is based on the basic colours yellow, red and blue (colours of the first order). The colours of the second order (orange, violet, green) are achieved by mixing the basic colours. All other colours come from mixing adjacent first and second order colours. If we imagine Otto Philipp Runge's colour-sphere to be a transparent body with black and white poles, with the pure colours on the equatorial zone and grey as the middle of the sphere, there exists the possibility of giving every point on and in the sphere a particular colour. The colour star shows the surface of the sphere. The sectors of the obscured side are cut open and projected into the plane of the illuminated notes. With the gradations of the twelve colours from black and white the colour star gives an overview and orientation of the totality of colour that is versatile in its applicability. This colour circle, developed in 1921, forms the basis of the Bauhaus theory.

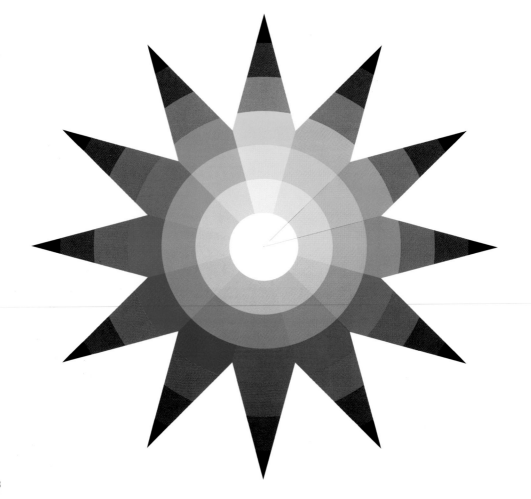

CHROMATIC CIRCLE, PRIMARY, SECONDARY AND TERTIARY COLOURS

On the computer we nowadays work with somewhat modified basic colours, yellow, magenta and cyan. The reasons for this are firstly technical: the red, green and blue areas of the spectrum are the best to filter out when reproducing, and the reversal colours (complementary colours) necessary for printing are as a result cyan, magenta and yellow. At the same time a mixture of these basic colours permits the printing of a relatively large colour expanse (well-known in the use of Desktop ink-jet printers and colour copiers).

In the illustrations below the chromatic circle customarily used today (24 divisions) is reproduced (see following page for exercise instructions). The circle contains both the primary colours of the light colours red, green and blue and the primary colours of the body colours cyan, magenta and yellow (also called varicolours). When composing/designing a chromatic circle the colours lying opposite each other should show the greatest contrast (see also complementary colours). The primary colours themselves cannot be achieved by mixing. On the other hand all other colours can be mixed from them. If one mixes 100% of each of two primary body colours the primary light colours (red, green or blue) appear simultaneously. And vice versa.

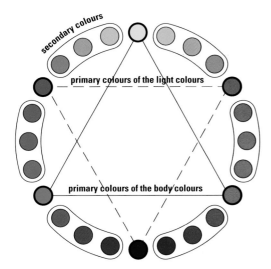

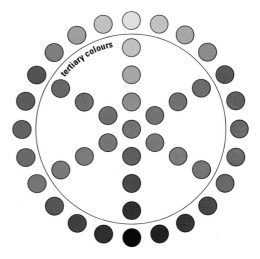

A chromatic circle consists of at least six segments and contains the primary colours of the light and body colours. The chromatic circles shown here consist of 24 segments and so each contain three secondary colours between the primary colours.

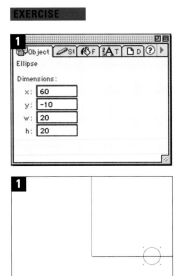

You should make a chromatic circle at least once in your life as a designer. This can be done in various ways: with brush and paint, with collages, or on a computer. In this exercise we realise a 12-part chromatic circle in Freehand. **1** Produce a circle 20 x 20 mm and, with the help of the "object panel", position it as stated (confirm with the enter key). **2** Select the circle and use the "transform panel" to rotate it by 30° (360° : 12 = 30°), using zero as the rotation centre (with x and y each 0) and 11 as the number of copies. Click "Apply" when you have entered the information. **3** After this, mix the CMYK primary colours: (% cyan / % magenta / % yellow): yellow 0/0/100, magenta 0/100/0, cyan 100/0/0 and assign to the circles as shown here. **4** Now mix the RGB primary colours: red, 0/100/100, green 100/0/100, blue 100/100/0 and fill the circles again as shown. **5** Lastly mix the colours in between with 100% and 50% respectively of two primary colours, e.g. amber, the colour between yellow and red, with 100% yellow and 50% magenta. Complete the circle in this way, group everything and move it on to the format. **6** If you do not already have the mixed colours in the colour panel, you can use the command "Xtras → colours → Name All Colours" as a control.

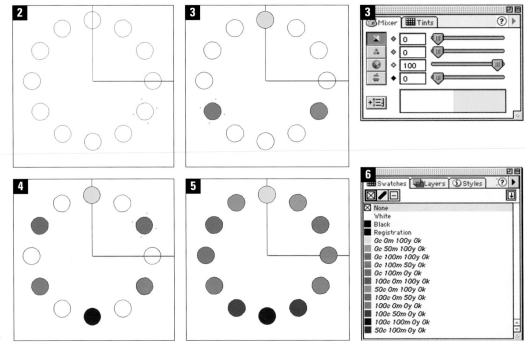

PRIMARY AND SECONDARY COLOURS

All colours that are mixed with less than 100% from two primary colours are called secondary colours – these comprise practically all those colours between the primary colours on the chromatic circle. Their distinguishing feature is that they keep their complete saturation (strength of colour) when mixed.

Produce the colour mixtures depicted below in 3 x 5 squares in QuarkXPress. Set **EXERCISE** CMYK as the colour model and untick the option "Spot Colour". Do not use the pre-defined colours red, green and blue but mix them yourself.

Name these colours corresponding to their proportions. You can see all the colours to be mixed in the screenshot on the left. Finally print colour separations (File → Print... → Tick "Separations") on a printer capable of postscript. If you have done everything correctly only three separations (cyan, magenta and yellow separation) should come out of the printer.

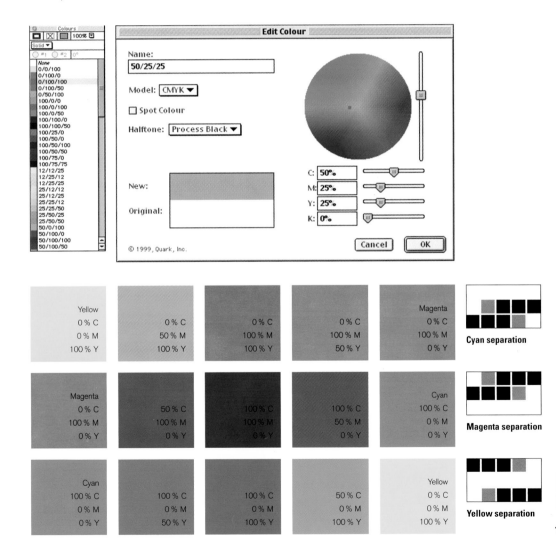

BRIGHTNESS AND SATURATION OF COLOUR

It is not only the achromatic "colours", or greys, that vary in brightness; colours themselves are also of different degrees of brightness. Some colours (such as yellow) are brighter than others (such as blue). But there are also varying grades of brightness within a single tone (see also page 100). These differences in brightness are variations of a fully saturated tone to white and black. Now use the chromatic circle on page 150 to create one or more brightness scales. **1** Clone the yellow circle, fill it in with white and place it exactly in the middle of the circle. Select the white and yellow circles. **2** Select the "Modify → Combine → Blend" command and then immediately enter the number of intermediate grades you want (two in this case) in the object palette (press the Return key to confirm). Highlight the resulting group (⌘ ⇧ G). **3** Select the yellow circle, clone it and place it above the circle (object palette: x −10; y 135). **4** Now create a "blend" with two intermediate grades as in step 2 from the yellow circle and the black circle. If you like, you can complete this by adding other degrees of brightness for other colours. In the result displayed below, the white and black points were reduced in size prior to "blending" and the black point was rotated around the zero point eleven times.

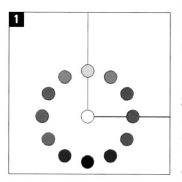

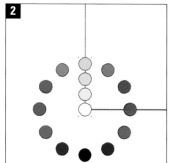

This is a much more difficult but worthwhile exercise: create a graded sequence of this kind using paints and a brush or paper cut from magazines.

The saturation of a colour is its degree of purity. Fully saturated colours are the primary **EXERCISE** and secondary colours in the chromatic circle (all colours containing no more than two primary colours). If a third component is added, the colour gradually dirties until it becomes a greyish brown. Colours made up of more equal parts of different components are less saturated. Complete the following exercise in Freehand to see how this works. **1** Use the chromatic circle from the exercise on page 150. Clone one of the circles, place it exactly in the middle and fill it with grey (either 50% black from the colour tones palette or a blended grey made up of the three primary colours: 50% cyan, 40% magenta and 40% yellow – see also page 108). Select one saturated circle and the grey circle. **2** Select the "Modify → Combine → Blend" command and then immediately enter the number of intermediate grades you want (two in this case) in the object palette (press the Return key to confirm). **3** Complete the chromatic circle as you like.

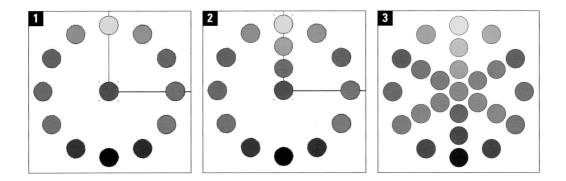

Of course, you can also create a graded sequence from a saturated to an unsaturated colour with other shapes or with paper cut from magazines.

TERTIARY COLOURS

Tertiary colours (also called unsaturated colours) are the result of blends containing all three primary surface colours (cyan, magenta and yellow, also called chromatic colours). These are colours with less saturation (chromatic power). Tertiary colours with a higher proportion of primary colours are darker, while tertiary colours with a lower proportion of primary colours are lighter. Most colours occurring in nature are tertiary colours. In the channel palette of Photoshop, you can recognise tertiary colours by the fact that they contain all three chromatic colour channels (and usually black as well). You can also find out the composition of a colour tone under CMYK by referring to the information palette.

You can use uniform ratios of chromatic colours to blend harmonic tertiary colour modulations.

100 % C 50 % M 100 % Y	75 % C 50 % M 75 % Y	50 % C 25 % M 50 % Y	25 % C 12,5 % M 25 % Y
75 % C 75 % M 100 % Y	50 % C 50 % M 100 % Y	25 % C 25 % M 50 % Y	12,5 % C 12,5 % M 25 % Y
50 % C 100 % M 100 % Y	50 % C 75 % M 75 % Y	25 % C 50 % M 50 % Y	12,5 % C 25 % M 25 % Y
75 % C 100 % M 75 % Y	50 % C 100 % M 50 % Y	25 % C 50 % M 25 % Y	12,5 % C 25 % M 12,5 % Y
100 % C 100 % M 50 % Y	75 % C 75 % M 50 % Y	50 % C 50 % M 25 % Y	25 % C 25 % M 12,5 % Y
100 % C 75 % M 75 % Y	100 % C 50 % M 50 % Y	50 % C 25 % M 25 % Y	25 % C 12,5 % M 12,5 % Y

Make a composition of each of the following tones: olive, ochre, terracotta, claret, aubergine, petrol. **1** To do this, find photographs or parts of photographs consisting mainly of tertiary colour elements in magazines or picture archives and scan them in small format, then open them in Photoshop. Select all ⌘A and copy ⌘C. **2** Triple the width of your canvas. **3** Enter the contents of the clipboard twice ⌘V (two new levels will appear) and use the "Move" tool (⊹) to move the content of the newest level to the right-hand edge of the image. **4** Do not alter the left-hand motif. Activate the level with the middle motif and select it using the "Transparency mask". Apply the "Filter → Pixelate → Mosaic...". **5** On the level with the right-hand motif, now use the command "Blur → Gaussian Blur..." and the filter "Distort → Wave..." with the settings shown.

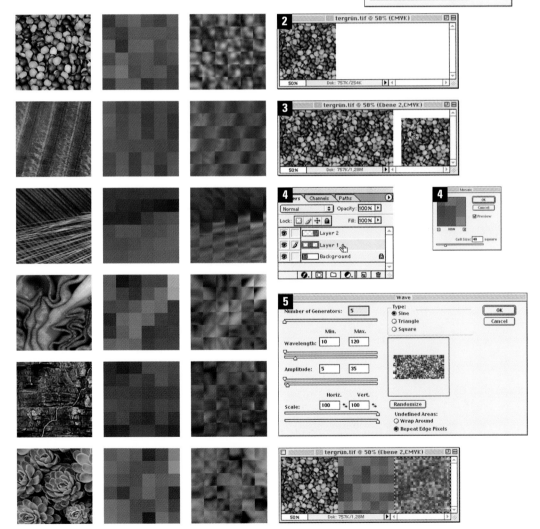

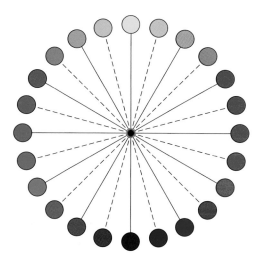

COMPLEMENTARY COLOURS – CONTRASTING COLOURS

Those colours lying opposite each other on the chromatic circle are those which show the greatest contrast. Each colour has its complementary colour – in this respect complementary colours are always colour pairs. The primary colour yellow for example is opposite blue, which is the mixture of the two primary colours cyan and magenta. Thus two complementary colours contain in total the same proportions of all primary colours. If such a complementary colour pair is mixed, the colours extinguish each other, resulting in grey.

In Photoshop try and take any colour image and invert it to its complementary colours using the command "Image → Adjust → Invert" (⌘ I). This reversal is the same as the colour negative in traditional photography.

When two complementary colours are mixed, it results in grey (try it out, for example in Freehand with the "Xtras → Create → Blend", as described on page 111).
Accordingly progressions between two complementary colours become grey in the middle.

COLOUR EFFECT – COLOUR CONTRASTS

Colour is not an absolute measurement. The impression of a colour changes with the surroundings. Design the following exercise in Freehand with the primary colours yellow, red, magenta, green, cyan and blue plus black and white and analyse and assess the different impressions given by the small colour fields.

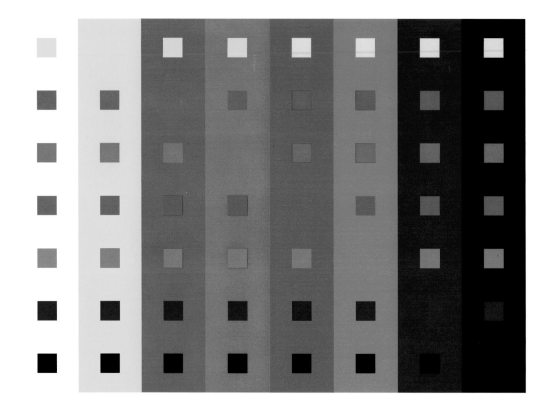

The most important observations would be as follows: the same colour appears lighter and brighter on a black background than on a white one. When complementary colours are put into a formal relation to one another (e.g. yellow and blue), the colour in the small square appears particularly bright. When colours from adjacent fields of the chromatic circle come together (e.g. red and magenta), their respective effect is muted. If there is no great difference in intensity (e.g. between red and green) a peculiar flickering will appear.

Johannes Itten recognised seven principle contrasts. "Each of these seven contrasts is so singular in its particular character and design value, in its optical, expressive and constructive effects, that the fundamental design possibilities of a colour can be recognised in them."

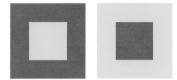

Pure colour contrast:
Juxtaposition of pure saturated colours
(black and white can heighten the effect)

Warm-cold contrast:
Juxtaposition of seemingly warm and
cold colours

Simultaneous contrast:
If the complementary colour is missing,
the eye creates the complementary colour
to each saturated colour

Quantity contrast:
Juxtaposition of two differently sized
colour planes

Light-dark contrast:
Juxtaposition of colours of differing
brightness or tone value

Complementary contrast:
Juxtaposition of colours that diametrically
oppose each other on the chromatic circle

Quality contrast:
Juxtaposition of saturated and unsaturated –
or bright and dim colours

EXERCISE Create compositions of 5 x 5 squares, in which you visualise contrasts using diverse colours (as well as colour tints). **1** Warm-cold contrast with the colours red, magenta, cyan, blue; **2** Warm-cold contrast with the colours green, cyan, blue; **3** Complementary contrast with the colours blue, orange, yellow;

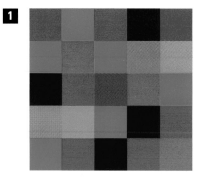
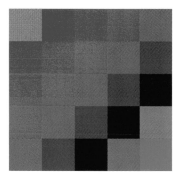

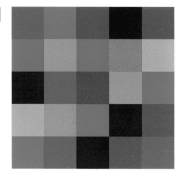
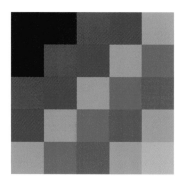

4 Dark-light contrast with different shades of grey; **5** Dark-light contrast with different shades of one colour; **6** Juxtaposition of different bright and dark colours; **7** Dark-light contrast with diverse colours; **8** Pure colour contrast.

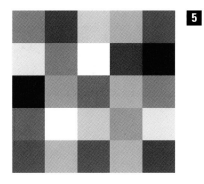

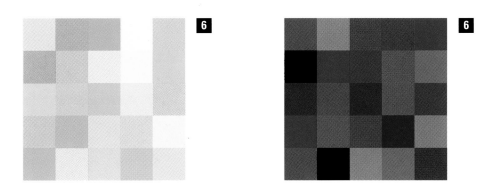

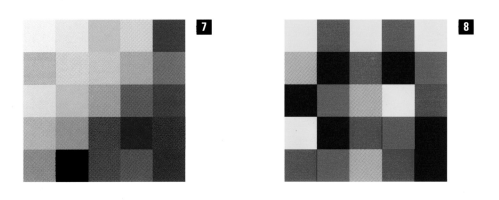

Find colour contrasts yourself. Open a new A4 document in Freehand or QuarkXPress. **1** Create nine planes (40 x 40 mm) by duplication. **2** Fill these planes with a primary colour, e.g. red. **3** Position a smaller square (20 x 20 mm) centred over each of these planes, and assign each of them a contrasting colour or tint – for the warm-cold contrast try blue. Label the nine contrasts that you have found. Design additional contrasts with other primary colours. Examine the colour effects. What comes forward, what recedes? Which colour combination has stronger contrasts? Which combination achieves utmost tension? Compare the observations with the contrasts described on page 159.

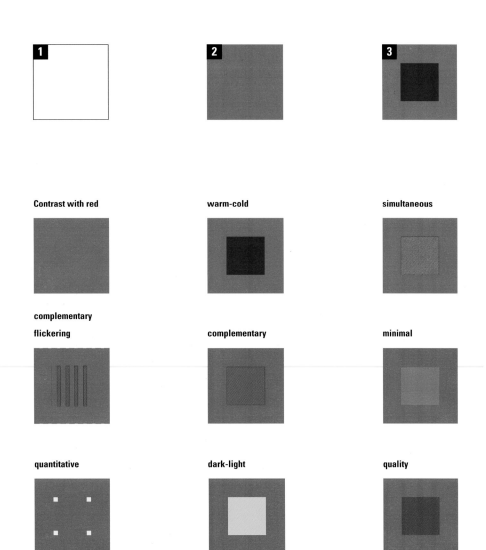

Contrast with red

warm-cold

simultaneous

complementary
flickering

complementary

minimal

quantitative

dark-light

quality

As in the last exercise, create colour planes. Fill them with colours of your own choosing and find a contrasting tone for each of them — each adhering to one of the colour contrasts discussed previously. Fill the small centred squares accordingly and label each contrast.

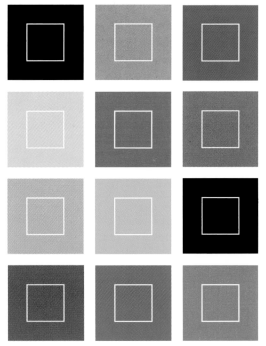

Go a step further and assign each colour one of these suggested terms. Consciously work with contrasts. With the colour contrast try to express each term-specific sensation. Heighten this sensation through the position of the term. Choose a sans-serif medium sober typeface (Arial, Frutiger, Akzidenz Grotesk, Univers). Enlarge and print the results and examine from a distance.

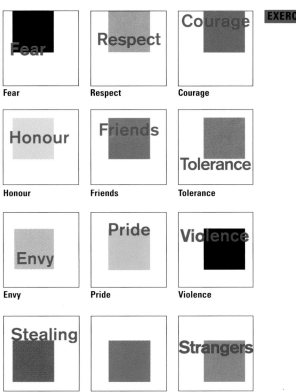

Fear   Respect   Courage

Honour   Friends   Tolerance

Envy   Pride   Violence

Stealing   Strangers

By duplicating a "cold" combination of four colours, create a square plane with 16 colour fields. Try to establish a warm-cold development from top left to bottom right by minimally altering the tints progressively. Develop different versions. The "cold-warm contrast enables very picturesque impressions and creates an atmosphere of musically sounding, unreal character." (Itten)

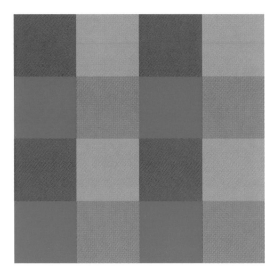

QUALITATIVE CHANGE – COLOUR COMBINATION AND EFFECT

By minimally changing a colour combination an overall effect can be changed drastically. Duplicate a composition of four squares a few times and change only one colour in each of them.

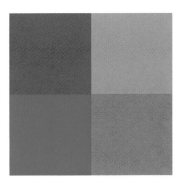
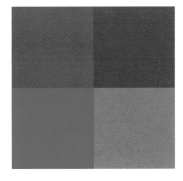

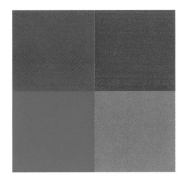

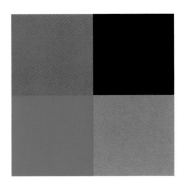
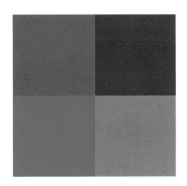

QUANTITATIVE CHANGE – PROPORTION AND EFFECT

The size relationship of differently coloured planes also play an important role in the overall impression. Create five rectangles of identical height and different width as shown. Fill these from a palette of five different colours. Duplicate the created strip a

few times and swap the colours around. Watch the diverse overall effects. Try to verbally express your sensations for each of the strips. Complete this exercise with different colour combinations.

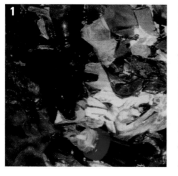

COLOUR ACCENTS

Complementary colours have an increased effect on each other. This does not mean that the colour pair has to match exactly, but that the colours should come from complementary fields. Furthermore, proportion plays an important part, that is the quantitative relationship of the complementary colours to each other. Thus effective accents can be achieved by matching "many" and "few".

Work with photographs or pictures which are predominantly in one colour. For example, all colours could be in a range of reds or the picture could be predominantly in blue or grey tones, as shown in the illustrations on the right. At the same time the colour co-ordination should be relieved by complementary colour accents. These can even be quite minimal complementary spots of colour. **1** Scan an appropriate photo, open it in Photoshop and duplicate it with the command "Image → Duplicate...". Save the original as a TIF format. **2** In the duplicate, create a new layer as background layer, either filling it with white or with a colour characteristic for the picture (double click on background layer, click "ok" in the "New Layer" dialog box, create a new layer and drag it to the bottom). Now isolate the complementary colour you have found in the picture layer by selecting the required tone with the pipette in the dialog box "Select → Colour Range..." (experiment with the "Fuzziness" setting in the dialog box). Generate a new layer from this selection by cutting (⌘ ⇧ J). Switch off the layer (click on the "eye" symbol) and save the document like this under a new name as a TIF. **3** Switch on the picture layer and switch off the layer with the isolated complementary colour and save the picture again as a TIF with another new name. Then you can load the three pictures into a Quark document in three picture frames, print it out and compare it. How does the picture look without the complementary contrast? (Cover up the original.) How does it look with its coloured "opponent"? Toned down complementary colour gradations may be found in the surrounding area which bring tension to the colour combination. Advertising photography frequently pushes the complementary contrast to its limits. It should be noted here that shape contrasts can compete with colour contrasts and sometimes overload the effect of the illustration.

In this exercise you are going to produce the reverse effect. You should use illustrations of similar colourfulness and if at all possible the same intensity. Set a colour contrast by adding a minimal shape or typographical addition. Note whether the given colourfulness leans towards a primary colour or if you are dealing with tertiary mixed tones. The complementary addition should acccordingly be saturated or covered. You can also achieve accentuation in the overall saturation through quality contrast or warm-cold contrast as well as with complementary contrast. Try to find harmonious tones so that the contrast effect is relatively unnoticeable. Also bear in mind the proportions. The particular effect is created when there is a quantitatively large gradient.

COLOUR AND SPATIALITY

Colours can specifically facilitate three-dimensional effects. On the one hand the brightness of the colours, as well as the background, plays a part in the three-dimensional effect – as you saw in the preceding exercise. The colours in themselves, however, also appear variably near or far. Spatially bluish, cool colours are inclined to recede, whilst reddish, warm colours seem to come forward. Furthermore perspective or isometric representations in themselves naturally evoke a three-dimensional conception.

EXERCISE Use the nine plane compositions from the exercise on page 103 and save them under a new name. Arrange five colours according to their brightness. Allocate colours to the squares in the compositions and try to achieve three-dimensional effects. Generate versions with different sequences of colour gradation.

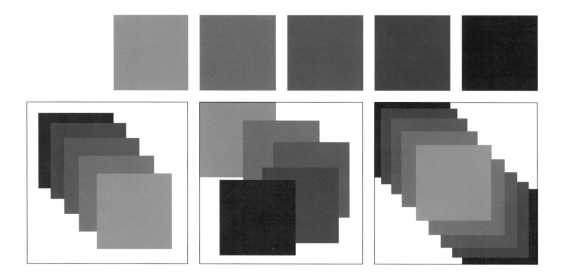

Through the brightness of colours a spatial effect is created and/or supported.

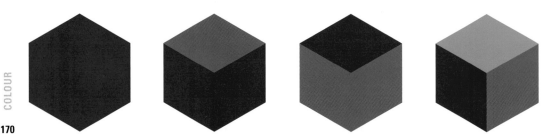

Examine the three-dimensional effect of warm and cold colours on the three simple geometric planes by exchanging the colours. What comes forward, what recedes, where is an unambiguous three-dimensional graduation? Create several practice sheets, each with six compositions in different colours.

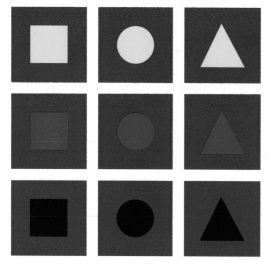

SHAPE AND COLOUR CONTRASTS

"One cannot make things with colour alone," (Kandinsky). In practical design work there is always an interchanging relationship between shape and colour. Different shapes of the same colour have different effects. Colour and shape effects can intensify or weaken each other. It also makes a difference whether a coloured plane is perceived as defined (surface colour) or virtually without beginning or end, as a plane colour (i.e. wall colour or sky). Colour surfaces perceived as unambiguously defined appear more compact and more coloured than those that lose themselves in "nothingness". In the same way small coloured planes appear to be more luminous than large ones. The edge treatment also plays a part. A blurred or otherwise unresolved edge of a surface colour makes the colour appear lighter than a sharply defined edge.

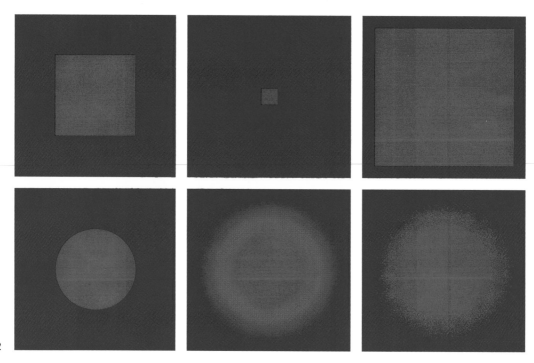

Generate square picture frames and fill them with a base colour of your choice. Starting with the three basic forms construct a square, triangle, circle and simple shapes with minimal variation so that the original shape is still recognisable. Position these centred on the picture frame. Then fill the shape, starting with your base colour taking into consideration the colour contrasts (see page 159). Try to achieve an incisive effect in each individual picture frame through a specific combination of shape and colour contrast. The shape contrasts strengthen the effect of colour contrast and vice versa. In this way, by deliberately analysing the contrasting effects (horizontal, vertical expansion, inner differentiation…) you can attempt to devise a trademark/logo.

COLOUR AND FONT

We use the same rules for coloured type on coloured backgrounds, i.e. the seven colour contrasts can apply here. If you are looking for good legibility, some combinations are better suited than others, and some are completely unacceptable. Examine the combinations shown here for legibility. Select the contrasts that help, those that are less suited and those that aren't up for discussion. Explain your decision and compare it with the overview shown on the opposite page.

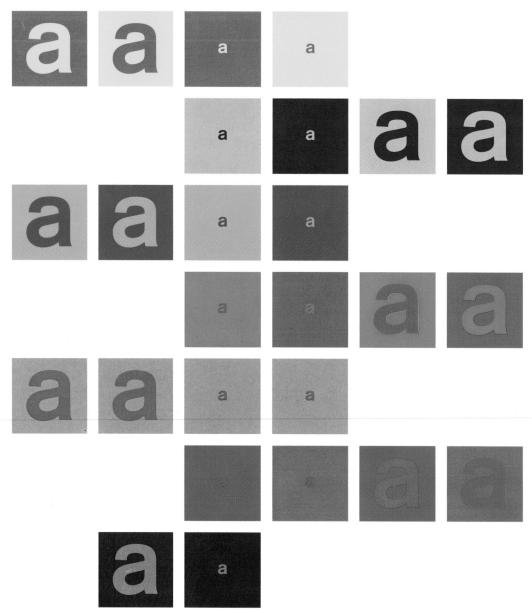

Black type on a white background has the best proximity impact.

Many think that red type has a high attention value, but actually red type is read less than text printed in black and white. Nowadays red type creates the impression of unimportant advertising.

Many think that red type has a high attention value, but actually red type is read less than text printed in black and white. Nowadays red type creates the impression of unimportant advertising.

In contrast, black print appears serious and informative.

Colour and Legibility (cf. Heller)

Black type on a yellow background has the best impact from a distance.

The impact of distance and proximity apply to different kinds of information. Distance impact is important for…

The impact of distance and proximity apply to different kinds of information. Distance impact is important for…

…information like street signs: for short messages that are commonly known.

…information like street signs: for short messages that are commonly known.

Distance impact has no bearing on longer texts of unknown information. These always have to be read in proximity. Here, colour can appear disruptive.

Distance impact has no bearing on longer texts of unknown information. These always have to be read in proximity. Here, colour can appear disruptive.

The smaller the lightness contrast of type and background, the lower the legibility.

The smaller the lightness contrast of type and background, the lower the legibility.

The more colourful a text (or background), the harder it is to read and the less important the information appears to be.

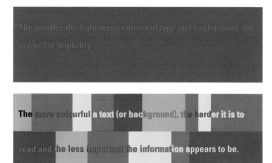

The more colourful a text (or background), the harder it is to read and the less important the information appears to be.

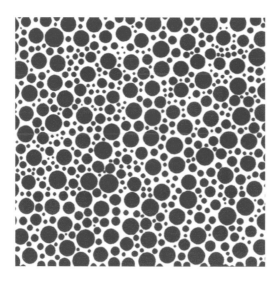

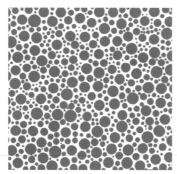

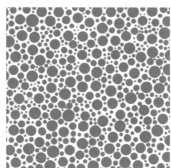

The famous eye test: here the sensation of colour is tested. The lower the saturation and the brightness contrast of the colours, the harder it is to read. If colours of virtually no difference in lightness (e.g. red and green) are combined, people with problematic colour differentiation cannot distinguish between the two (left).

COLOUR IRRITATIONS

Completely regular geometrical patterns provoke a movement of the eye, making it appear as if the pattern is moving (flickering). Colours can heighten this impact.

TRANSPARENT COLOURS

Transparency (translucent, see-through) stems from overlaying colours that are not completely opaque. Transparency (with mono-coloured planes) can be achieved by "overprinting" the watery-thin offset print colours. By mixing these translucent colours one creates new tones in between. For the colours in question, the "overprint" option in Freehand or QuarkXPress has to be ticked. The effect is not visible on screen, but only later in the offset print process or on a colour proof.

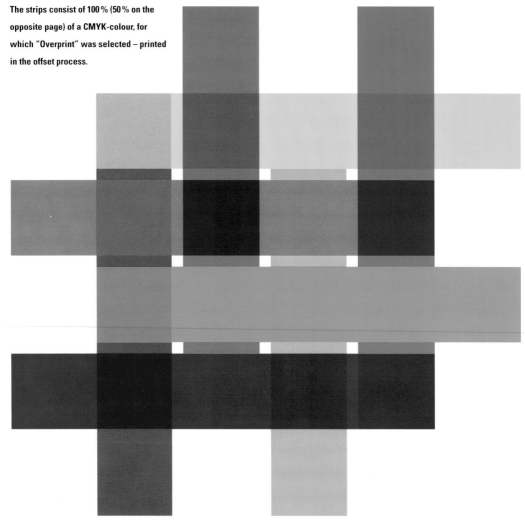

The strips consist of 100% (50% on the opposite page) of a CMYK-colour, for which "Overprint" was selected – printed in the offset process.

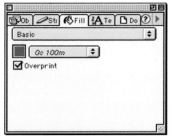

By default, colours in most DTP programs are set to "Knockout" with automatically defined amounts (apart from black which normally should "Overprint"). This can be manually changed for individual colours in the "fill" dialog box in Freehand and respectively with "Edit → Colours... → Edit Trap" in QuarkXPress. It is advisable to print colour separations.

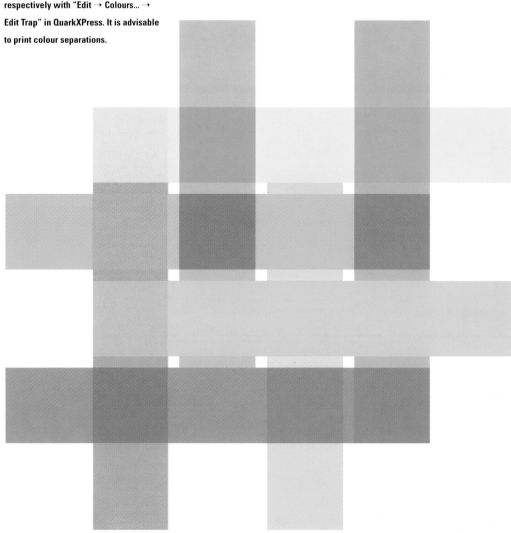

TRANSPARENCY AND HARMONY

Overlaying transparent colours creates a variety of new colours. As long as the colours used are not too far apart in the chromatic circle, it can create harmonious colour blends. Create a pattern of overlapping, transparent colours. Use four base colours that are adjacent in the chromatic circle (here shades of green and blue). **1** In Freehand, with the help of a grid create four strips and fill them with these four colours. **2** Clone and move them around within the grid until a rectangular plane is completely filled. **3** In order to create an irregular colour distribution, you can subsequently select individual strips and give them different colour fills (if needed, use "Xtras → Colours → Name All Colours"). **4** Export the graphic as an .eps ("File → Export") and open it in Photoshop. Set the resolution for the purpose of this exercise to 72 dpi (normally 300 dpi for print) and determine the desired size. **5** Create a new layer and move all the way to the bottom and fill with a pastel tint of the same colour range. **6** Duplicate this layer at least three times. **7** Now experiment by moving the layer contents horizontally or vertically ("Move Tool" and arrow keys) and play around with the layer options (e.g. "Multiply") and opacity settings.

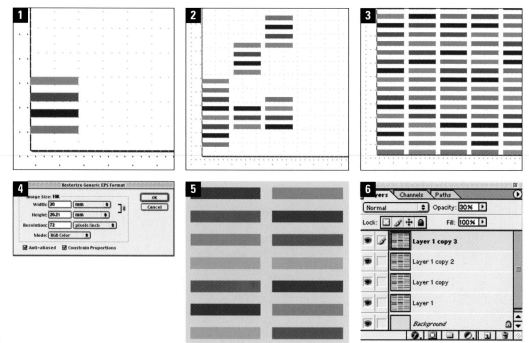

COLOUR

7

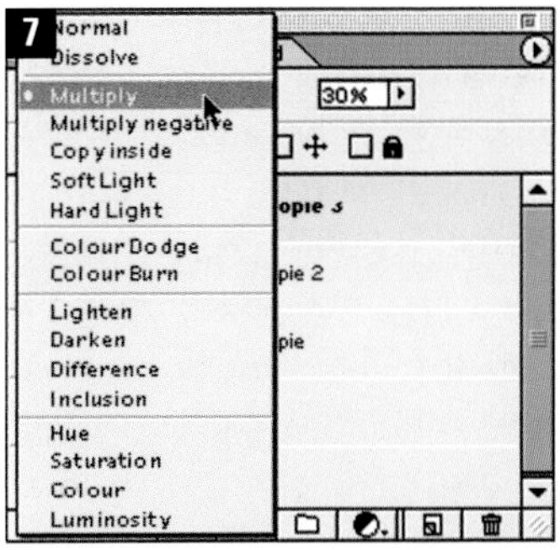
Normal
Dissolve
Multiply
Multiply negative
Copy inside
Soft Light
Hard Light
Colour Dodge
Colour Burn
Lighten
Darken
Difference
Inclusion
Hue
Saturation
Colour
Luminosity
30%

7

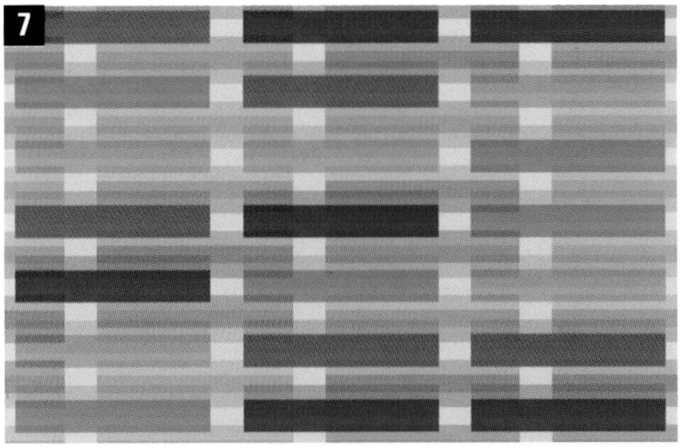

7

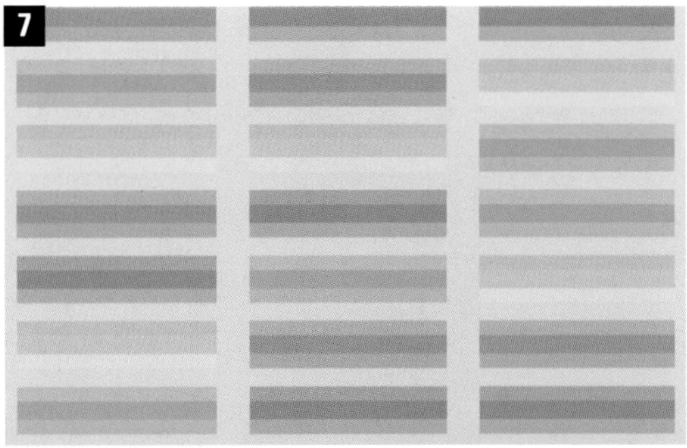

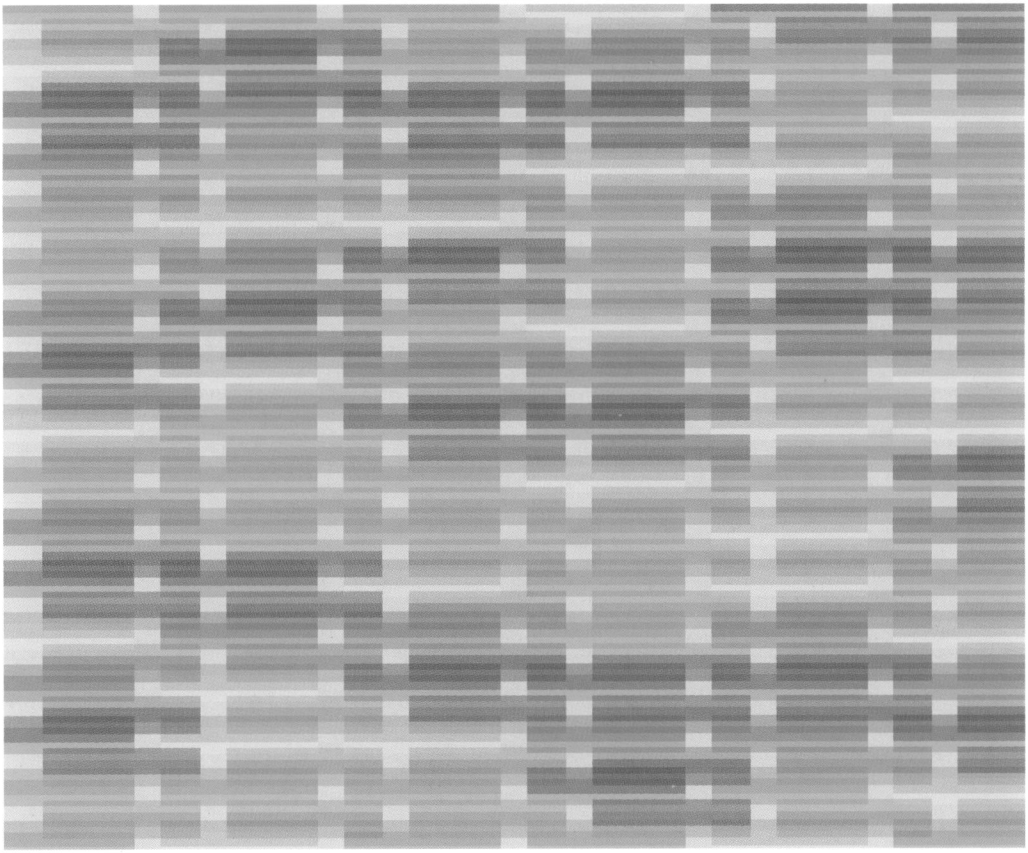

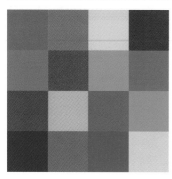

Proximity harmony

HARMONY: CHROMATIC-ACHROMATIC, TONE-IN-TONE, PROXIMITY

In general what we understand by harmony is unison and agreement. Harmony is more calming or agreeable than energising and is not just felt subjectively. One or more common features underlie colour harmonies. Every single colour harmonises with black or white (colourful-uncolourful harmony, see page 139). Colours of a modulation series, e.g. uniform gradations of several colours to white, black and grey, are considered to harmonise (tone in/on tone harmonies, see also page 110) – in the same way light tones go with white, dark tones with black and muted tones with grey. In addition mixtures of two colours, colours of the same intensity, colours of the same saturation, are experienced as harmonious (likewise tone in/on tone harmonies). Arrangements of colours in small colour tone steps, such as usually occur in nature, e.g. the various green tones of fields and meadows (see the following exercise) are defined as neighbouring harmonies. At the same time colours with which one can recognise/feel a systematic sequence also harmonise, e.g. with spectra. As a result harmonies can also lie in colour contrasts, e.g. an arrangement of several primary colours (colour in itself contrast).

Select colour images with harmonious colour tones from magazines or picture archives as described above, and scan whole or details of the pictures as small format. Create an A4 document in Photoshop and set a grid. Now place the scanned pictures each with 4 x 4 grid divisions and trim them accordingly into squares. With the pipette ("Eyedropper Options → Point Sample → 5 x 5 Pixels Average") choose 16 typical harmonising colour tones from each picture and fill each with square planes. Arrange the results according to their intensity.

1

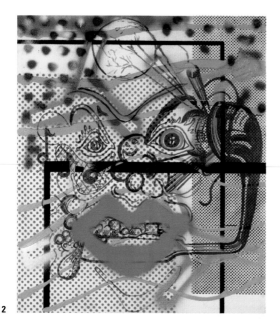

2

1 Sigmar Polke, "Konstruktivistisch"
(Constructively), 1968, colour dispersion on
canvas, 150 x 125 cm.
2 Sigmar Polke, "Dr Berlin", 1969–74,
colour dispersion, varnish and spray on
textile. (Printed by kind permission of the
artist © Sigmar Polke.)
3 Tom Wesselmann, "Still Life No 20", 1962,
collage and assemblage of paint, paper,
wood, light bulb, switches etc. 104; 14 x 121;
92 x 13; 97 cm (© ProLitteris, 2002, 8033
Zürich).
4 Max Bill, "Hexagonal Plane Around
2 Squares", 1969, 200 x 200 cm, oil on canvas.
(Printed by kind permission of Dr. Jakob Bill.
© ProLitteris, 2002, 8033 Zürich.)

3

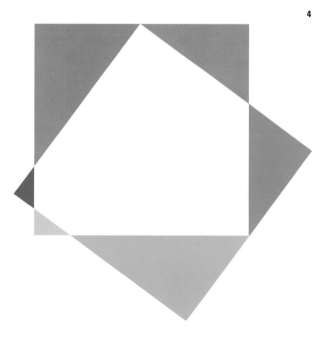

In Sigmar Polke's work the rasterised image is a recurring theme. Here, as an ironic statement on art history, a screened and distorted reproduction by Piet Mondrian (the de Stijl group) becomes the basic grid and simultaneously explores the technological era of screen and offset print.

For his still life, Tom Wesselmann also uses a reproduction by Mondrian, combined with various objects of home furnishing. The "Mondrian" next to the cabinet continues the modular shelf design on the two-dimensional plane.

Max Bill, an exponent of the "Konkrete Kunst" (direct art) movement, uses mathematical-geometrical experiments to create "colour-formal" designs.

MODULAR CONSTRUCTIONS

In preceding chapters we looked at basic principles of design. In the exercises on point, line and area, body, space, form and colour, light and dark, the technical possibilities of graphic programs were used to investigate phenomena in detail, providing valuable visual experience.

In this chapter, we look at more complex constructions, at concepts of visual design that allow us to unite all the pieces into a whole. Artistic compositions on surfaces are characterised by the fact that their individual components are arranged in a particular structure on a defined format. Now we move on to work with the entire breadth of visual materials, typefaces and manifestations of shape. Contrast of form and colour and the laws of proportion now come into effect. The basis for this work is the arrangement of visual elements within a grid system. Practice with grid modules opens up a further field of experimentation.

Brightness, halftone, greyscale

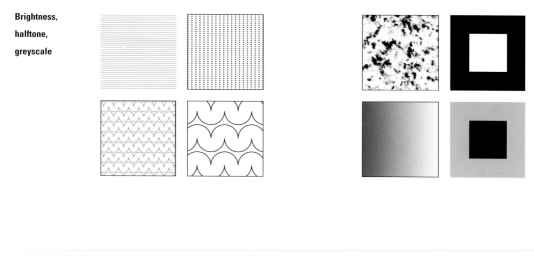

Primary, secondary, tertiary colours

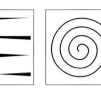

Basic elements:
dot, line, plane

Media:
drawing, graphic
b/w photo, text,
colour photo, painting

**Geometrical
primary shapes:**
triangle,
square,
circle

INVISIBLE NETS – GRID – STRUCTURE

"Structure is fundamentally understood as the construction of a framework (see internal itemisation). This can mean the internal makeup of a form or equally the framework of a visual composition," (Lupton, Miller). An invisible grid gives us a foothold in our composition. Like sorting things into shelves and cupboards, the individual design elements are fitted into the grid. Everything is carefully stacked so that the corners are aligned and the edges of the pile form a straight border. Invisible grids pervade the layout systems of well-designed contemporary publications. Even the seemingly chaotic layouts of the innovative designer are based on ordered layout structures and deliberate design concepts.

The practice with the materials presented here must not and should not lead to a prescriptive, static expectation of results. Rather, the exercises, which represent only a cross-section of the broad spectrum of design methods, are intended as a stimulus to lead you on to an examination of artistic methods. Practical implementation using graphic programs provides training in routine use of the technology, as well as valuable experience in visual perception and design. The practice with manual drawing on the one hand (sketches, drafts) and the application of graphic software on the other (copying, modifying, transforming, filling in), provided there is self-critical monitoring and analysis of the processed material, forms the basis for the translation of specific contents into a comprehensible and stimulating visual language. Using graphics programs you can easily construct and arrange grid structures to work with.

Structural means:

surface grid, perspective grid, axial division of the plane, 3D grid

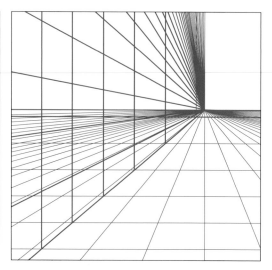

Take to heart the instruction not just to look at the visual material you produce on the computer, but to print it out regularly and view it from a distance. At the least, view the prints of your work standing up, placing them on your desk or on the floor. Only in this way can you gain an overview and discern the internal structure of a design. A trained eye is sensitised to this kind of visual perception and will notice disturbances and clashes as well as the characteristics of a successful piece of work. Even a layout that uses a grid can become overloaded. It might be that the individual parts are positioned disjointedly within the design area, or that despite the visual elements working separately, the overall appearance is lacking any proportion in the format. Aim for minimal solutions: only clear and simple messages will be understood. Most amateur products are overloaded. The effect of contrasts of form and colour is over-used and therefore cancels itself out. Closer observation of these sorts of tussles of form and colour reveals the use of clichés that will disturb the trained eye. Much experience is required before visual and textual materials can be used to deliberate effect with proper consideration of the powers that bear on visual design, and before content can be convincingly translated into visual language.

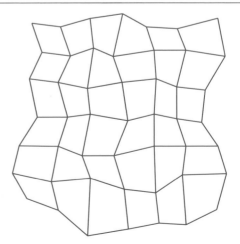

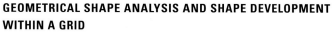

GEOMETRICAL SHAPE ANALYSIS AND SHAPE DEVELOPMENT WITHIN A GRID

The primary shapes circle, square and triangle form the starting point. Their external and internal shape may be modified through geometric deconstruction using the grid. The aim is to develop a new shape, for example for a corporate identity. A symbol or logo should convey a message in both content and form. Even the decision as to its basic shape, whether round or square, is a statement in itself (see page 39). The covering of individual cells, the division of the whole, the displacement, removal or addition of parts – all represent a work method that opens up a new visual field of experience. At the same time, routine use of Freehand provides training. The segmentation or break-up of the basic shape along the lines of the grid should lead either to the development of an autonomous symbol, or to the deconstruction of the shape proportional to the design area. The latter can be applied to all types of format, for instance a portrait format for a book or landscape format for a poster. Each primary shape that has been deconstructed can be broken up in different formats. Initially, you should pursue strictly graphical experiments, in other words with linear or monochromatically filled picture frames. Before you move on to photo material or linear textures, it is recommended that you practice with various shades of grey.

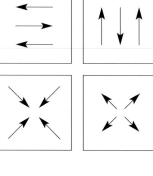

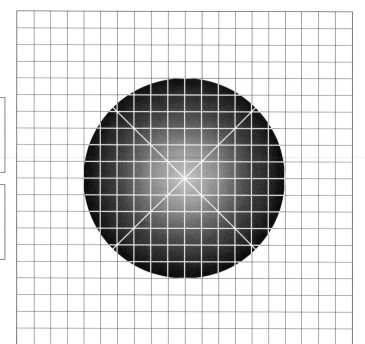

Elementary ways of breaking up the source element in the grid: horizontal, vertical, centred towards the centre,

centred towards the outside, irregular

Then you can start to use colour, or to try implementing area results linearly and vice versa. Photo material should only be brought into play at the very last. The following pages contain suggestions for practice as well as procedural instructions (see page 194).

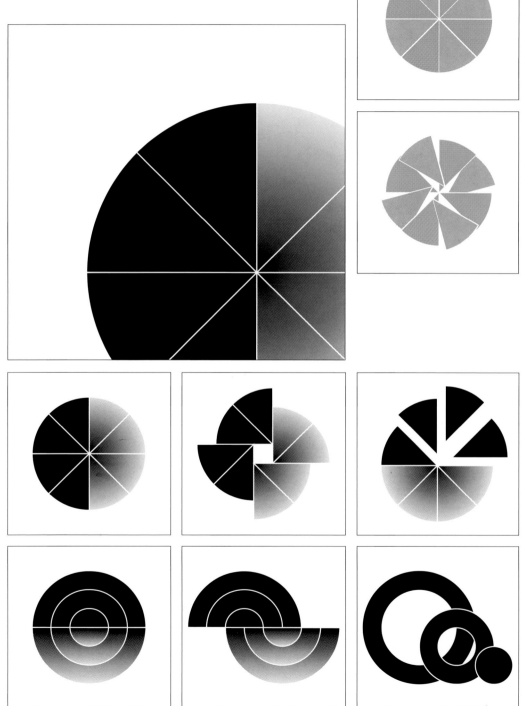

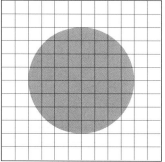

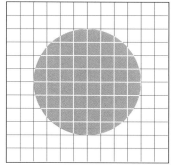

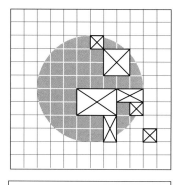

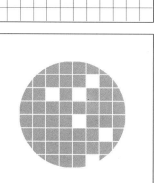

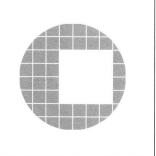

Dissolution of form within the grid by covering of individual grid elements. The shape breaks up irregularly.

The covers can be duplicated, deleted or grouped at will.

Covering of larger parts of the basic shape with other shapes (rectangle, strip, circle segments, undulating lines).

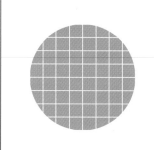

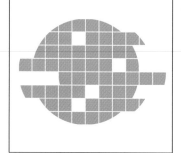

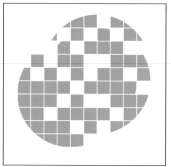

Horizontal and vertical division of the basic shape in the grid.

By moving individual or joint parts the basic shape changes horizontally.

Change of the basic shape through horizontal and vertical distortion.

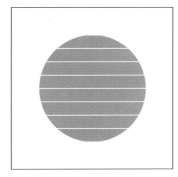

Horizontal division in the grid.

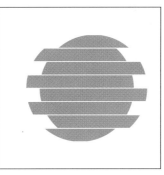

Horizontal displacement of the segments creates an agile shape.

Displacing evenly can create the impression of two shapes.

Star-shaped division of the circle into eight segments. Various new formations develop with displacement and rotation of single or multiple segments as well as a separation through colour.

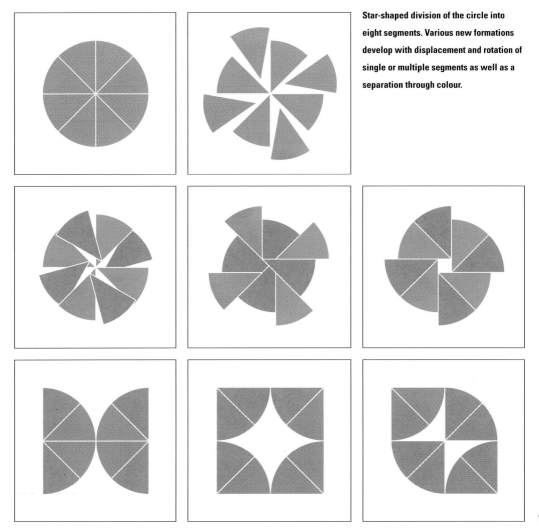

GRID AND GUIDES

1 Create a new square-format document in the Freehand program ("Window → Inspectors → Document → Custom"). **2** Freehand allows you to work with an automatic grid. This is an indispensable tool that reduces workload and guarantees precision. It is activated through "View → Grid → Show". Custom grid spacing can be set through "View → Grid → Edit…".

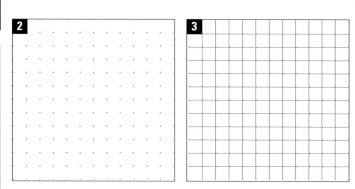

3 It is often helpful to construct an additional grid containing guidelines ("Guides"), not least because these can later be converted into normal lines and used for the precise division of a primary shape (see section "Changing shapes by dividing"). Horizontal and vertical guides are created through "View → Guides → Edit…". If you enter a value for "Enlarge" (spacing), the number is calculated automatically. You can activate the guides through "View → Guides → Show". Additionally it is recommended that you lock the guides ("View → Guides → Lock"), so that they can't be displaced accidentally when working.

CHANGING SHAPES BY MASKING

4 In your Freehand document, create a primary shape such as a square or a circle, in a size and colour of your choice, and position it within the grid. Cover parts of the shape through the positioning of "masks" – white-filled, square elements that are orientated on the grid. These may be duplicated, deleted or shifted as desired. The arrangement of the masks within the design area allows the form to be broken up systematically. Pay attention to the dynamics you create.

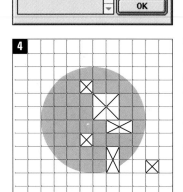

MODULAR CONSTRUCTIONS

CHANGING SHAPES BY DIVIDING

5 There are various possibilities for dividing shapes in Freehand. For our exercises the following procedure is particularly appropriate: Choose "View → Guides → Edit…", select all the guides that run over the shape that is to be divided, and click on "Apply" – in this way the guides are converted into normal lines. The line-width is unimportant. **6** Now select all lines and the primary shape as well. Apply the command "Modify → Combine → Punch" – the lines act as a guillotine and slice the shape into corresponding parts. Unselect (⇥), select the parts anew and displace them separately or in groups along horizontal or vertical axes. The same principle may of course be applied to other shapes and arrangements of lines, e.g. the star-shaped division of a circle.

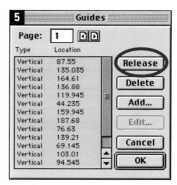

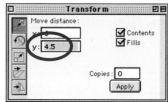

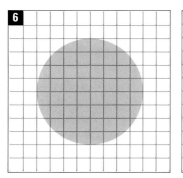
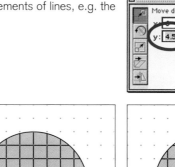
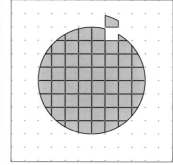

CHANGING SHAPES BY PUNCHING

Cutting a shape out of a closed object is called punching. **7** Position a second shape as a cut-out form over the primary shape. Select both objects and choose the command "Modify → Join" or "Modify → Combine → Punch". The uppermost shape is cut out of the lower shape. For every shape resulting from the cut out, two objects are required: the external primary shape and the cut-out shape.

For exact displacement of irregular parts use the "Transform" panel. Use "Move distance" by entering numerical values in accordance with the grid into the X and Y textfields.

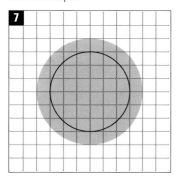
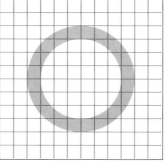
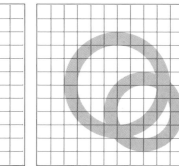

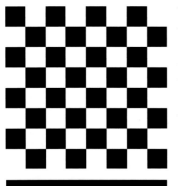

TRANSLATION – TRANSFORMATION

A large part of design work is concerned with assigning sentiments to artistic contents and, conversely, in translating terms that express sentiments into an abstract language of colour and shape. Whichever type of product we are dealing with, in artistic design, subject matter on a rational, notional level is conveyed to a purely artistic level that can be perceived only abstractly. This process is termed "translation". There are always a number of possibilities for translation, in which intuitive and systematic approaches can be used in turn. In the quest for a design solution, pinning one's hopes on finding a unique, ingenious answer is counterproductive. On the contrary, a sense of development should be discernable in every design. Development usually ensues in a number of stages – so even a sketch or draft of the layout counts. A path is trod from notion to form, from form to deconstruction, eventually arriving at a composition. When working with grids, everything is interconnected. By allowing the initial shape and the intermediary stages of the design process to remain discernable, more attentive observation is stimulated.

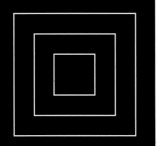

A grid offers good opportunity to divide a shape systematically into component parts. Working with a grid, displacement, distortion or reduction of a primary shape, for example, allows direction and movement to be implemented in such a way that the original shape remains recognisable, though a totally new formation has emerged. Depending on the brief, this can allude to itself or its surroundings. Important for the result is that the viewer is able to comprehend the choice of shape, and that the desired sentiment is expressed.

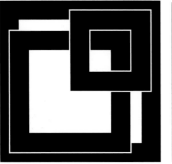

(DE)CONSTRUCTION IN THE GRID

Create a new A4 document in Freehand and activate the automatic grid. Define the grid line spacing (see page 194). Create one of the primary shapes (square or circle) in a size of your choice and position it in the grid. Divide the shape geometrically, i.e. in the form of a circle, star, square, using horizontal or vertical lines based on the grid, as described on pages 194–195 (cover, divide or cut out). Make several copies of the pieces as starting points for different versions and their stages of development, and arrange these on an A4 page. Try to implement the following notions through removing or displacing the different pieces: "Breath", "Tension", "Reflection" and "Connection". In the result, the primary shape should still be recognisable in rudimentary form. You can achieve this by just covering the individual pieces and/or displacing them minimally. The aim is to develop a suggestive symbol (e.g. a logo for a corporate design). Also work without surroundings to the design area. In the coming exercises, vary shades of grey and colour. With each addition of a further design facet, new forms of contrast come into effect. Take care that the effects do not cancel each other out (see pages 74 and 159 for effects of contrast).

COMBINING SHAPE AND TYPOGRAPHY

Now combine the shapes you have modified geometrically with a letter. Look up page 76, which deals with letters as shapes in a format. Using the text tool, create a letter, transform it into strokes ("Text → Convert to Strokes") and fill it in with white. This letter can now be rotated, inclined, scaled to size or merged with the other parts of the design as an object. Work with a grid and with "slanting guides".

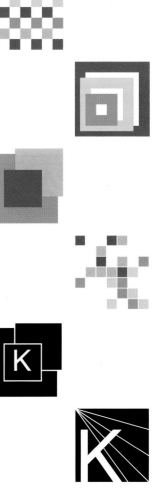

COMBINING SHAPE AND IMAGE

Deconstruction of the primary shape through masking or dividing, whilst at the same time changing colour or image in the course of the same exercise is not appropriate. Rather, formal solutions, assignment of colour and work with typeface and visual materials should be carried out in successive steps, so that endeavours can be viewed and analysed without impediment on different levels of perception. **1** The next step might be to import a photo or photo detail in TIF format into Freehand, where it is positioned behind the shape in question and cut (⌘X). The shape is then selected and the picture pasted from the clipboard into the selected shape using the command "Edit → Paste Inside". The example on the left shows the picture pasted into the shape at the back.

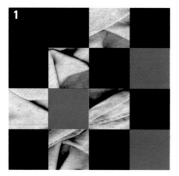

COMBINING SHAPE, IMAGE AND TYPOGRAPHY

1 Fill a geometric shape with photographic material as described above. In this way an internally differentiated complementation to the external shape is created. Break up the shape in one of the ways outlined previously. Break it up in such a way that the original shape remains recognisable and a dynamic form is created. **2** Combine the shape with some text. Create axes to assist the proportional and harmonious organisation of all parts of the picture. Work with a line of text as a headline and with one or two text frames with smaller dummy text. Position this text frame in relation to the primary shape. The aim of this exercise is to achieve a dynamic arrangement of the parts in relation to one another.

A FEW WORDS ON TYPOGRAPHY

Typography is the art of designing well-proportioned, reader-friendly texts. Methods of text design are many and varied: Font, orientation, size and their combination, the spacing of letters, words and lines, contrast and emphasis, the spacing of paragraphs and columns, micro-typography – as the list shows, this subject contains enough to fill at least one other book. There are already many books that examine the various aspects of typography in detail. Reference works are listed in the bibliography on page 254. For this reason, the extensive subject of typography receives only cursory mention in this book in as far as it is of artistic interest. Intensive study of general principles of visual design will certainly throw up many parallels with typography, as well as giving you a foundation that will help in the discernment and aesthetic evaluation of text design. A further piece of advice: if you work with these exercises using text, try to use clear, simple fonts without embellishments, e.g. a sans-serif linear-antiqua such as Arial, Helvetica or Futura. As a matter of course, limit yourself to using a maximum of two different fonts.

1

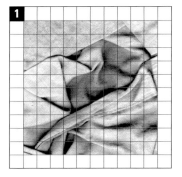 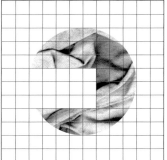 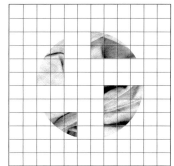

2

SHAPE AND TYPE

It is not advisable to break down the basic shape by masking or dividing and altering colours and images all at the same time. It is much better to complete each step separately, i.e. try out purely formal solutions, colours, fonts and images one by one, so that you can examine and analyse your possible solutions in isolation, considering their effects on various levels of perception.

SHAPE AND TYPE

It is not advisable to break down the basic shape by masking or dividing and altering colours and images all at the same time. It is much better to complete each step separately, i.e. try out purely formal solutions, colours, fonts and images one by one, so that you can examine and analyse your possible solutions in isolation, considering their effects on various levels of perception.

SHAPE AND TYPE

It is not advisable to break down the basic shape by masking or dividing and altering colours and images all at the same time. It is much better to complete each step separately, i.e. try out purely formal solutions, colours, fonts and images one by one, so that you can examine and analyse your possible solutions in isolation, considering their effects on various levels of perception.

SHAPE AND TYPE

It is not advisable to break down the basic shape by masking or dividing and altering colours and images all at the same time. It is much better to complete each step separately, i.e. try out purely formal solutions, colours, fonts and images one by one, so that you can examine and analyse your possible solutions in isolation, considering their effects on various levels of perception.

TANGRAM – PLAYING WITH SHAPES

The Chinese "Tangram" is a jigsaw puzzle that differs from European puzzles in that the number and shape of the pieces is set. The Tangram consists of seven pieces, so-called elementary shapes, which are formed through the geometric division of a square. The illustration on the left shows how the seven pieces must be arranged in order to recreate the square. Without the picture the task is by no means straightforward! The idea of the Tangram is to create other shapes from the seven elementary geometric pieces – a rectangle or triangle, a parallelogram, a trapezium or free forms for example. Of interest to us, aside making up these shapes, is the substitution of pieces with photo material or the omission of particular pieces, similar to the "covering" technique used in the previous exercises. Countless possibilities for variation in the deconstruction of shape emerge.

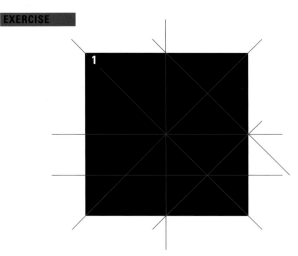

1

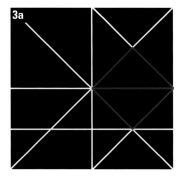

3a

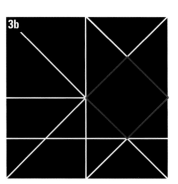

3b

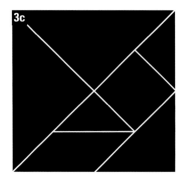

3c

1 Create a new A4 document in Freehand. Activate the automatic grid function and set the spacing to 5mm. Position a 100 x 100 mm square in the centre of the grid and fill it in black. Draw division lines in another colour across the square as illustrated – the division lines must be continuous without breaks – and slightly over the edges of the square. 2 Select all the lines as well as the primary shape. Divide the square as described on page 195 using the command "Modify → Combine → Punch". It is unavoidable that the primary shape will be divided up according to the lines into more parts than actually required. 3 Select the shapes that belong together and use the command "Modify → Combine → Union", until all parts are merged as in illustration 3c. 4 Make several duplicates of the page and its contents. Deactivate the automatic grid function if necessary. Play around with the pieces of the puzzle, shifting and rotating them to create rearrangements of the square on the theme "Beware wild animals", taking care that the rudiments of the basic shape remain recognisable. Experiment with various page formats by taking a larger frame as a boundary to your format. Bring lines of text into the composition. Print out your results and compare them (see next double page). 5 Using further duplicates, experiment with colour and picture cuttings, and with themes such as "explosion", "fallout", "reflection" or "fracture". 6 Alternatively, you can print out several copies of the Tangram square and cut out the pieces by hand. Lay out the pieces on a white surface and experiment with different shapes.

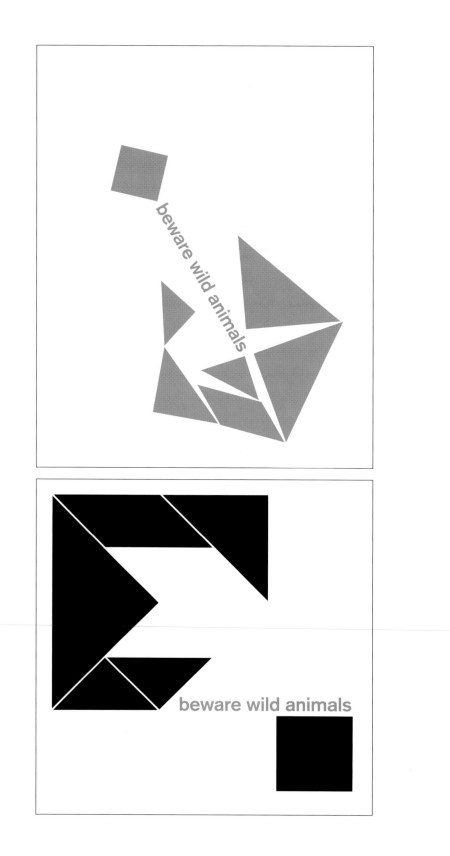

beware wild animals

beware wild animals

wild
wild
wild

beware wild animals

USING A GRID TO DEVELOP A LAYOUT

Each piece of printed material, each Web project has its own layout demands – there are never two the same. But the task is always to find a design solution that is appropriate for the contents and message. In this there are some common fundamental practices, some general rules that must be regarded and some areas of procedural overlap. We will now demonstrate the development of a layout using this book as an example. The first step is to make some fundamental decisions concerning the purpose of the printed matter, its projected readership, its intended "lifetime" (short expiry date or lengthier timeframe), the scope of its content in relation to the number of pages, its purpose (i.e. flyer, book, catalogue), as well as budgetary demands. In our case, we are dealing with a book, which means that we will design double page spreads and must consider the binding. Its print space is relatively small in relation to the given number of pages (256), in a format that measures 160 x 230 mm.

The consequence of this is that the amount of text is high relative to the format, requiring the margins to be relatively slim (between 10 and 15 mm). It is hardly necessary to state the necessity of using a

The illustrations always show the left-hand page of the double page spread.

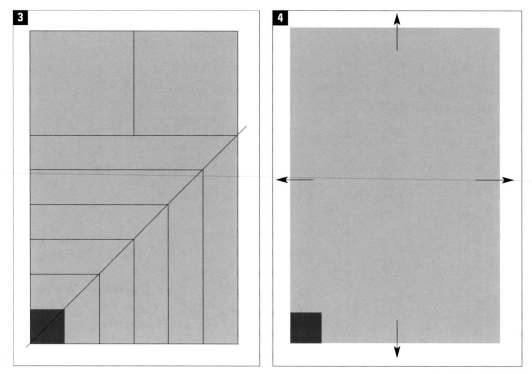

grid here. The advantages of this tool have already been stated on page 188. **1** As most of the exercises in this book are based on square design areas, it makes sense to use a square for the basis of the grid. Also to consider, is how large the smallest illustration must be, in order that it can still be discerned; this is set at 20 mm. **2** Now first ideas on the division of the page are sketched. How many of these squares fit into the page whilst allowing enough spacing: 6 across and 9 down – a proportion that is generally considered balanced (2:3). Some possibilities for variation are tested with a grid. **3** Only now is it time to use the computer: The document format is set up in QuarkXPress. The division into 6 x 9 grid squares is checked – if the margins prove insufficient, a version with 5 by 7 cells and somewhat larger squares could be tried. **4** Then the size of the print space is calculated. In doing this, preliminary column width/cell spacing must be considered, so that the illustrations are later well-spaced. 6 squares and 5 spaces result in a width of 135 mm (20 x 6 = 120 + 3 x 5 = 15); 9 squares and 8 spaces result in a height of 204 mm (20 x 9 = 180 + 3 x 8 = 24). The preliminary print space is laid out in grey and placed on the double-page template. (First double-click on the master page in the "Document Layout Panel".) Shifting the grey areas around allows you to find a position that is optically appropriate. **5** Enter the resulting spacing (whole numbers if possible) as well as the number of columns using "Page → Master Guides…" (see page 206).

There are also different ways to create a grid, for instance taking the page format as a basis to determine the print space and then dividing it up.

Going against the aforementioned method it is also possible to take the spacing of the body copy as a basis for the page grid.

Rule of thumb for the column gutter width: Width of the lower case "m" and "i"

→ mi ←

in the font that is used for the body copy. If the spacing or leading is more than 140 % of the type size, the numerical value of the gutter width can be larger than or equal to the spacing.

too low

too high

without tension

acceptable

The bottom margin should always be larger than the top margin to prevent the page content from visually sliding down (see page 75). The inner margins are classically narrower to prevent the pages from optically breaking apart. However, with books that have extremely narrow margins, like this one, it is advisable to make the inner margins wider as the content might otherwise disappear in the binding which reduces legibility.

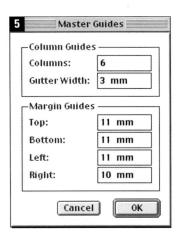

5 | Master Guides

┌─ Column Guides ─
Columns: 6
Gutter Width: 3 mm

┌─ Margin Guides ─
Top: 11 mm
Bottom: 11 mm
Left: 11 mm
Right: 10 mm

[Cancel] [OK]

6 Unfortunately, in QuarkXPress there is no option to allow the automatic calculation of the horizontal grid lines. These guides must be laid out on the template manually. The spacing must therefore be checked in the "Measurements Panel" (zoom in if necessary). **7** At this stage it is recommended that you check the result again, by trying out various page divisions using grey areas or blocks of texts in QuarkXPress. **8** It is also helpful to take a page, substitute the print space and guides with lines, and print out a number of copies. These print-outs are highly useful for sketching or scribbling on, or for pasting picture cut-outs on to. It also circumvents the "fear" of the empty white page. However curious it might seem, limiting our scope allows our creativity to unfold all the more.

When designing double pages, never view these separately. An open book with its opposite pages views like a mirror-image. Try to create a dynamic sense of balance; this does not mean you should aim for symmetry, rather you should aim to balance various contrasts, e.g. large, few and light on one page and small, many and dark on the other – always under due consideration of the homogeneity and integrity of the publication.

5

6

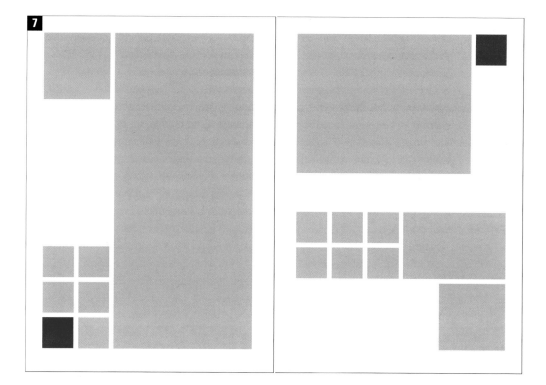

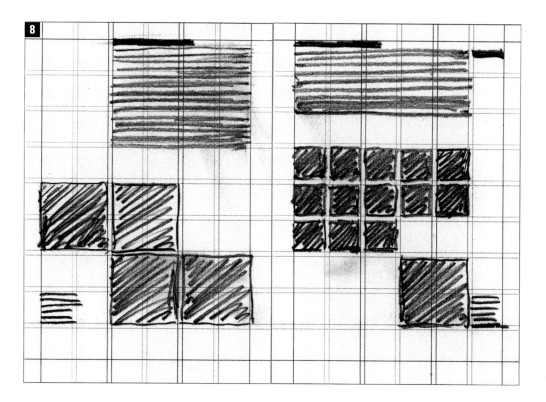

SETTING UP THE BASELINE GRID

Working with a basic grid guarantees concise, consistent layouts (indispensable for multi-column texts), whilst also representing an enormous reduction in work. The upper and lower edges of the print space must correspond to the grid lines. In our book the aim was also to align the line of the text with the bottom edge of the illustrations – in other words the lower edge of a grid cell. As the grid size is already set, fixed line spacing is the result, something which can be a disadvantage, for example when larger font sizes are used (see below for alternatives). **1** After the font(s) and font size(s) have been set under due consideration of the typographical concept, a sample text is loaded into a text frame. The text is formatted in the chosen font, in our case this is 9 point with desired line spacing of 13 point. This leaves us with 5 lines in a grid segment that is 23 mm high. The precise line spacing can be calculated from the grid segment height (23 mm): 5 lines = 4.6 mm. The values for the line spacing are entered only in the "Measurements Panel" for the time being – this can be done in millimetres (value and "mm") or in point size (1 pt = 0.35277 mm/4.6 mm : 0.35277 mm = 13.039 pt).

2 If one now creates a picture frame and lays this out, as the text frame, on the upper edge of the print space, it will become apparent the text does not yet sit within the grid. For this reason we shift the text frame upwards, until the line of the fifth line of text is aligned with the lower edge of the first grid cell. **3** Then, a horizontal guideline drawn with the ruler becomes the line of the first text line, and the value is read in the "Measurements Panel" – this is the foundation for the basic grid. This value, along with the calculated line spacing, is entered under "Edit → Preferences → Document → Paragraph". The option "Lock to Baseline Grid" can now be selected in the style template for the flow text.

2 er having determined the font and type size according to typographical rules, a sample text can be loaded into the text box. Initially, the text will be formatted according to the determined font, type size and spacing. After having determined the font and type size according to typographical rules, a sample text

3 After having determined the font and type size according to typographical rules, a sample text can be loaded into the text box. Initially, the text will be formatted according to the determined font, type size and spacing. After having determined the font and type size according to typographical rules, a sample text

ALTERNATIVE GRID DEVELOPMENT

This is another method for construction of a side grid with an integrated baseline grid that allows line spacing to have priority: the number of lines intended to fit into the print space and the number of desired grid lines are coordinated. First though, the number of spacings which later separate the illustrations must be subtracted from the number of lines. Then the number of lines is divided by the number of grid cells. Example for 9 grid cells: 53 lines − 8 spacings = 45 lines: 9 grid cells = 5 lines per grid cell. Example for 8 grid cells: 47 lines − 7 spacings = 40 lines : 8 grid cells = 5 lines per grid cell. However, this will only work if the number of lines minus the spacings produces a multiple of a whole number, and consequently the calculation produces a whole number.

The top and bottom edge of the print space should be in accordance with the baseline grid.

After having determined the font and type size according to typographical rules, a sample text can be loaded into the text box. Initially, the text will be formatted according to the determined font, type size and spacing. After having determined the font and type size according to typographical rules, a sample text

After having determined the font and type size according to typographical rules, a sample text can be loaded into the text box. Initially, the text will be formatted according to the determined font, type size and spacing. After having determined the font and type size according to typographical rules, a sample text

Simple, yet unsatisfactory is the alternative whereby the start of the baseline grid (blue) is set at the same height as the top edge of the print space (red) as the first line of text will be on the second baseline. This method will mean that illustrations positioned next to the text will stand out of the text block.

A better solution: Open a text box with the same height as the print space and fill with sample text. Highlight all (⌘A) and increase the line spacing by .10 steps (click on the spacing arrow in the "Measurements Panel" while keeping the alt-key ⌥ pressed). Check the position of the lowest text line until it lines up with the bottom edge of the print space and the mean line of the top-most line of text lines up with the top edge of the print space. Now adjust the baseline grid accordingly.

TEXT FORMATTING

The aim of formatting text is to bring together the various contents and make them one homogeneous whole; to present content correlations, lead the eye and optimise legibility. There are countless possibilities in order to achieve this. Content-related text can be laid out in one or more, larger or smaller shapes (text blocks) with equal or differing typographic colour. Essentially, formatting is a combination of alignment, spacing, kerning as well as the choice of font or typeface (see page 30 and 104).

TEXT ALIGNMENT

The most frequently used form of alignment is justified or left-aligned text. The closed form of justified text appears static which quietens the impact and increases concentration. Hence it is one of the most popular forms of alignment. Newsprint also uses justified text; here the varying sizes and position of text blocks creates dynamic and rhythm which counteracts fatigue. With justified text, in contrast to other methods of alignment, it is necessary to vary the word spaces (or even kerning) in order to achieve equal line length (see page 105). Hence, wider text columns have longer lines and offer more satisfactory results than narrow ones. However, greater quantity of text and lines that are too long hamper "finding" the next line and induce fatigue. Lines with up to 60 characters are perceived as ideal. With less than 30 characters per line, the word spacing will become too irregular and left-aligned text is advisable.

Text aligned left or right should have rhythm to the lengths of the lines. The development of stairs and curves disturbs the rhythm. With left-aligned text, it is advisable to use program preferences that prevent the lines from becoming too irregular (in QuarkXPress: "Edit → H&Js... → Auto Hyphenation"). Often it is also necessary to break words manually, although this shouldn't lead to too many consecutive word breaks (3–4 maximum). If possible, break words at the roots. Left-aligned text is often used in the setting of poetry, or longer headlines and pull-outs. Because of its restricted legibility right-aligned text should only be used for example to align captions with the corresponding image or margin notes with the left-aligned body copy.

Justified

Aligned left

Aligned right

MODULAR CONSTRUCTIONS

Edit Hyphenation & Justification

Name:

Standard

☑ Auto Hyphenation
Smallest Word: 4
Minimum Before: 3
Minimum After: 3
☑ Break Capitalised Words

Hyphens in a Row: 3 ▼
Hyphenation Zone: 20 mm

Justification Method

	Min.	Opt.	Max.
Space:	95%	100%	150%
Char:	0%	0%	0%

Flush Zone: 0 mm

☐ Single Word Justify

Cancel   OK

Centred alignment can be dignified and elegant –
but also static, conservative, boring and without
tension. Accordingly, centred alignment can be
justified for ceremonial and representational designs.
On the contrary, asymmetrical alignment offers
substantially more design potential for structure,
contrast and tension and hence appears more modern
and dynamic. If you do want to work with centred text,
you should also pay attention to the vertical shape of the
text block, which should be narrow rather than wide.

Centred alignment can be
dignified and elegant – but also
static, conservative, boring and
without tension. Accordingly,
centred alignment can be
justified for ceremonial and
representational designs. On
the contrary, asymmetrical
alignment offers substantially
more design potential for
structure, contrast and tension
and hence appears more
modern and dynamic. If you do
want to work with centred text,
you should also pay attention to
the vertical shape of the
text block, which should be
narrow rather than wide.

Rhythm disturbance

Left-aligned text: stairs

Left-aligned text: curves

Centred: too many equally long lines

Centred: too many equally short lines

FORM, TYPOGRAPHY AND LAYOUT

The layout grid accommodates all text and images, as well as all other design elements like planes and shapes. As long as it isn't solely formal and informative print design, but also concerned with the integration of images, it leaves room to manoeuvre. Tints, when used like images can increase the dynamics and create visual contrast to the body copy. Using type size, leading and alignment, text blocks can be formatted (see page 210) or shaped. Another possibility of alignment is the form setting: Text can flow into a visible or invisible shape or take on a shape by itself; aligned to a contour of a shape text can flow around it. Another way of text alignment is the form setting: Text can flow into a visible or invisible form or can by itself take on a form; aligned to the contour text can flow around a shape or alongside it. With form setting, shapes have to be assigned a "runaround" – the gap between the object and the text – and often the word breaks have to be manually fixed. Even photographic material can be scanned and loaded into forms. Design a layout grid with 36 equal planes, separated by an even gutter width (see page 205) and arrange text and shapes within this grid.

Text can flow into a shape or take on a shape itself. Text can flow into a shape or take on a shape itself. Text can flow into a shape or take on a shape itself. Text can flow into a shape or take on a shape itself. Text can flow into a shape or take on a shape itself. Text can flow into a shape or take on a shape itself. Text can flow into a shape or take on a shape itself. Text can flow into a shape or take on a shape itself. Text can flow into a shape or take

Text can flow along a shape.

Text can flow into a shape or take on a shape itself. Text can flow into a shape or take on a shape itself. Text can flow into a shape or take on a shape itself. Text can flow into a shape or take on a shape itself. Text can flow into a shape or take on a shape itself. Text can flow into a shape or take on a shape itself. Text can flow

The layout grid accommodates all text and images, as well as all other design elements like planes and shapes. As long as it isn't solely formal and informative print design, but also concerned with the integration of images, it leaves room to manoeuvre. Tints, when used like images can increase the dynamics and create visual contrast to the body copy. Using type size, leading and alignment, text blocks can be formatted (see page 210) or shaped. Another possibility of alignment is the form setting: Text can flow into a visible or invisible shape or take on a shape by itself; aligned to a contour of a shape text can flow around it.

Another way of text alignment is the form setting; Text can flow into a visible or invisible form or can by itself take on a form; aligned to the contour text can flow around a shape or alongside it. With form setting, shapes have to be assigned a "runaround" – the gap between the object and the text – and often the word breaks have to be manually fixed. Even photographic material can be scanned and loaded into forms. Design a layout grid with 36 equal planes, separated by an even gutter width (see page 205) and arrange text and shapes within this grid. The layout grid accommodates all text and images, as well as all other design elements like planes and shapes. As long as it isn't solely formal and informative print design, but also concerned with the integration of images, it leaves room to manoeuvre. Tints, when used like images can increase the dynamics and create visual

The layout grid accommodates all text and images, as well as all other design elements like planes and shapes. As long as it isn't solely formal and informative print design, but also concerned with the integration of images, it leaves room to manoeuvre. Tints, when used like images can increase the dynamics and create visual contrast to the body copy. Using type size, leading and alignment, text

The layout grid accommodates all text and images, as well as all other design elements like planes and shapes. As long as it isn't solely formal and informative print design, but also concerned with the integration of images, it leaves room to manoeuvre. Tints, when used like images can increase the dynamics and create visual contrast to the body copy. Using type size, leading and alignment, text

The layout grid accommodates all text and images, as well as all other design elements like planes and shapes. As long as it isn't solely formal and informative print design, but also concerned with the integration of images, it leaves room to manoeuvre. Tints, when used like images can increase the dynamics and create visual contrast to the body copy. Using type size, leading and alignment, text

The layout grid accommodates all text and images, as well as all other design elements like planes and shapes. As long as it isn't solely formal and informative print design, but also concerned with the

The layout grid accommodates all text and images, as well as all other design elements like planes and shapes. As long as it isn't solely formal and informative print design, but also concerned with the integration of images, it leaves room to manoeuvre. Tints, when used like images can increase the dynamics and create visual contrast to the body copy. Using type size, leading and alignment, text blocks can be formatted (see page 210) or shaped. Another possibility of alignment is the form setting: Text can flow into a visible or invisible shape or take on a shape by itself; aligned to a contour of a shape text can flow around it. Another way of text alignment is the form setting: Text can flow into a visible or invisible form or can by itself take on a form; aligned to the contour text can flow around a shape or alongside it. With

form setting, shapes have to be assigned a "runaround" – the gap between the object and the text – and often the word breaks have to be manually fixed. Even photographic material can be scanned and loaded into forms. Design a layout grid with 36 equal planes, separated by an even gutter width (see page 205) and arrange text and shapes within this grid. The layout grid accommodates all text and images, as well as all other design elements like planes and shapes. As long as it isn't solely formal and informative print design, but also concerned with the integration of images, it leaves room to manoeuvre. Tints, when used like images can increase the dynamics and create visual contrast to the body copy. Using type size, leading and alignment, text blocks can be formatted (see page 210) or shaped. Another

The layout grid accommodates all text and images, as well as all other design elements like planes and shapes. As long as it isn't solely formal and informative print design, but also concerned with the integration of images, it leaves room to manoeuvre. Tints, when used like images can increase the dynamics and create visual contrast to the body copy. Using type size, leading and alignment, text blocks can be formatted (see page 210) or shaped. Another possibility of alignment is the form setting: Text can flow into a visible or invisible shape or take on a shape by itself; aligned to a contour of a shape text can flow around it. Another way of text alignment is the form setting: Text can flow into a visible or invisible form or can by

itself take on a form; aligned to the contour text can flow around a shape or alongside it. With form setting, shapes have to be assigned a "runaround" – the gap between the object and the text – and often the word breaks have to be manually fixed. Even photographic material can be scanned and loaded into forms. Design a layout grid with 36 equal planes, separated by an even gutter width (see page 205) and arrange text and shapes within this grid. The layout grid accommodates all text and images, as well as all other design elements like planes and shapes. As long as it isn't solely formal and informative print design, but also concerned with the integration of images, it leaves room to manoeuvre. Tints, when used like images can increase the dynamics and create visual contrast to the body copy. Using type size, leading and alignment, text blocks can be formatted (see page 210) or shaped. Another possibility of alignment is the form setting: Text can flow into a visible or invisible shape or take on a shape by itself; aligned to a contour of a shape text can flow around it. Another possibility of alignment is the form setting: Text can flow into a visible or invisible form or can by itself take on a form; aligned to the contour text can flow around a shape or alongside of it. With form setting, shapes have to assigned a "runaround" – the gap between the object and the text – and often the word breaks have to be manually fixed. Even photographic material can be scanned and loaded into forms. Design a layout grid with 36 equal planes, separated by an even gutter width (see page 205) and arrange text and shapes

The layout grid accommodates all text and images, as well as all other design elements like planes and shapes. As long as it isn't solely formal and informative print design, but also concerned with the integration of images, it leaves room to manoeuvre. Tints, when used like images can increase the dynamics and create visual contrast to the body copy. Using type size, leading and alignment, text blocks can be formatted (see page 210) or shaped. Another possibility of alignment is the form setting: Text can flow into a visible or invisible shape or take on a shape by itself; aligned to a contour of a shape text can flow around it.

Another way of text alignment is the form setting: Text can flow into a visible or invisible form or can by itself take on a form; aligned to the contour text can flow around a shape or alongside it. With form setting, shapes have to be assigned a "runaround" – the gap between the object and the text – and often the word breaks have to be manually fixed. Even photographic material can be scanned and loaded into

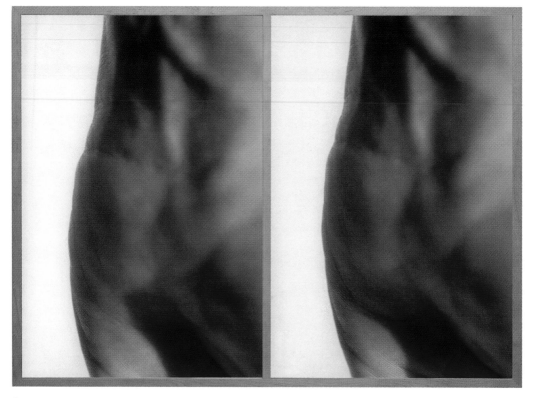

1

1 Thomas Florschuetz, "Diptichon # 157", 1995/96, cibachrome, 155 x 206 cm. (Printed by kind permission of the artist.)

2 Eva-Maria Schön, "With The Finger From Left To Right And Back", 1992, Projection on to the hand. (Printed by kind permission of the artist.)

3 Nanaé Suzuki, from the series "Self Portraits", 2000/2001, Photography (blurred with mask), 30 x 40 cm, 30 x 40 cm, 26 x 37 cm. (Printed by kind permission of the artist.)

The work of Thomas Florschuetz, Eva-Maria Schön and Nanaé Suzuki have their origins in traditional photography. Thomas Florschuetz works with consciously chosen large-scale image details. Eva-Maria Schön photographs the projection of one of her works of ink on to the hand. Nanaé Suzuki produces images with intentional motion blur. An interesting image result does not depend on technical perfection or digital trickery, but on the intensive consideration of the chosen theme, the in-depth examination of the recording medium and last but not least a clear compositional solution.

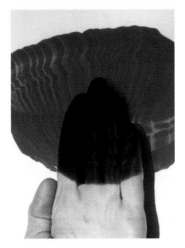

2

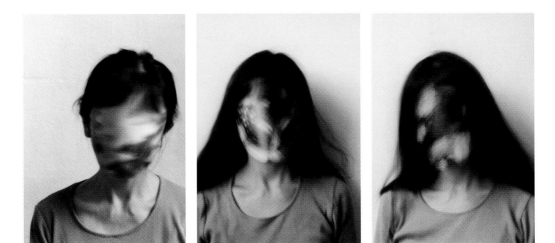

3

IMAGE ORGANISATION

By what criteria should imagery be chosen? How can imagery be organised on the image plane? What creates the right tension in an image composition or arrangement? How can different visual elements be sensibly put into relation with each other? There is no one generally satisfactory answer to all these questions, but various strategies can aide the development of sensible image concepts. The "action areas" introduced on the following pages represent a small selection out of a great possible number of strategies that the so-called creatives (graphic designers, artists) use to access imagery.

COLLECTING AND ARRANGING

Any design application has a cause or a theme which needs to be visually communicated. How do I approach a theme? How do I narrow down a theme? To translate this content into a visual language needs planning and research. To search for imagery and information is top-most on the list. The theme, a contextual formal impulse, is taken as a starting point in the search, collection and arrangement of material – incidentally this also applies to scientific research. In the realm of visual design, the subject of consideration needs to be accurately researched and captured by eye and camera or pen; it needs to be recognised in publications, in the museum, in the street or wherever you may be. Everything that can help with the subject needs collecting: pictures, photographs, texts, incidental material.

What is at the heart of a subject? What is its message? The subject (e.g. a product or the aims of a community) is scrutinised from various angles: psychologically, socio-politically, economically, atmospherically, formally and aesthetically. To find some orientation amidst the abundance of possibilities, the material has to be categorised and accordingly archived. Containers for this can be small sketch books, a folio with separation sheets as well as databases and folders on the computer. "Bearing in mind the psychologically basic fact that man looks for order – even loves order – he (Peter Jenny) sets the task of finding and recognising order especially where initially it seems to be absent (e.g. in 'chaotic', 'informal' structures). Here, the search for order, the creative act of finding initially invisible forms and meanings can at the same time become a kind of projectional test (…)," (Rainer K. Wick on Peter Jenny).

PLACING AND PRODUCING IMAGE MATERIAL

Imagery can be found in magazines, holiday-photo albums, advertising brochures or folios with children's drawings. However, imagery often has to be produced for a cause, i.e. it needs to be photographed, drawn or mounted. In Photoshop, images can for this purpose be retouched, manipulated or be subjected to colour changes. Image details can be copied and pasted into and integrated with other images. These are all possibilities to visualise a message or mood and to translate it into a design solution. Consider the act of searching, collecting and arranging not merely as project-specific, but, similarly to hand drawing as a continuous process.

COMBINING – MATCHING – MANIPULATING

The search and archiving of imagery is followed by the process of selection. Individual pictures, clippings, details and text segments are taken from the archive and examined for compatibility. A series of architectural shots can be used as background for a deconstruction of form. To search photographs for similarities in form or to create colour relations between image sequences of widely differing motifs is a way to develop homogeneous design from an eclectic mix of images. The conscious and transparent setting of a visual centre of gravity is always at the core of this process. Which relations become visible with a certain selection?

– Similarities: similar shapes, similar colours, similar structures
– Repetition: ornamental complexities
– Reflections: negative/positive relationships – overlays – transparency
– Perspectives: point of view, position
– Dimensions: formats, spatial relations
– Actions: motion sequences in nature or technology
– Content-specific relationships: image-linguistic additions

The possibilities of finding images are endless. Finally there are also the DTP programs that further enhance the process of image development. The changing and reconstructing of existing imagery into new compositions, the sequential arranging of images or the creation of backgrounds – all this aides the development of new communication contexts. But within this great variety of possibilities also lies the danger: the digital production techniques resemble a jungle of offers in style and taste that are only too tempting to get lost in. This is why you should always focus on a tiny detail and work on it intensively for some time. Run the results out on your printer and then look at them and criticise them individually. Our examples on the following pages and an orientation at the above discussed criteria should inspire and challenge you to design your own image concepts.

Designing image concepts is not about perfect picture quality. Even unfinished, incidental work can be suitable and welcome to an overall visual solution. Furthermore, high resolution images can hinder the creative process by considerably slowing down the computer through the sheer quantity of data to be processed. In this light, develop your image concepts in a sketch-like fashion: scan with low resolution and experiment on a small scale. This is why we consciously refrain from giving any advice on scanning, complex image retouching, artworking and file preparation for print. Please see our recommended reading list on page 254 for more information.

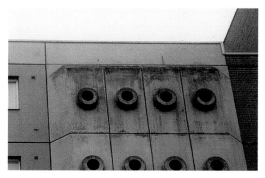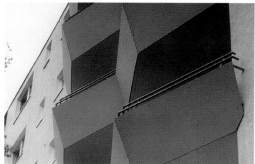

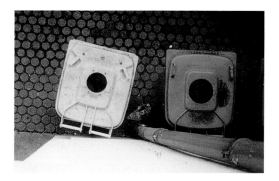

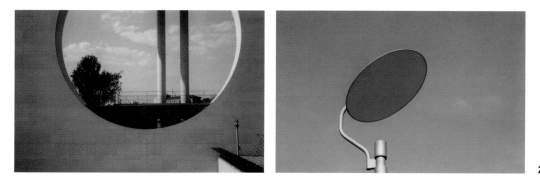

Image relationships can be created by presenting complete pictures as well as corresponding shots of details and clippings from the master image.

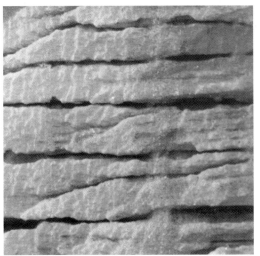

Another way to create image relationships is the inversion of
particular details from positive to negative black-and-white
images or by using backgrounds. These types of elevations seem
digressive and similar at the same time – they are versions of the
same form and structure.

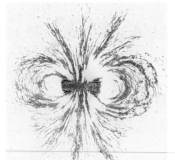

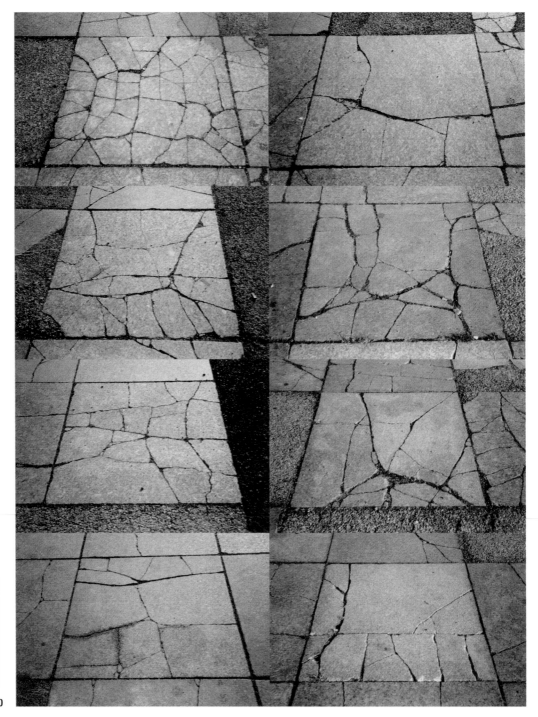

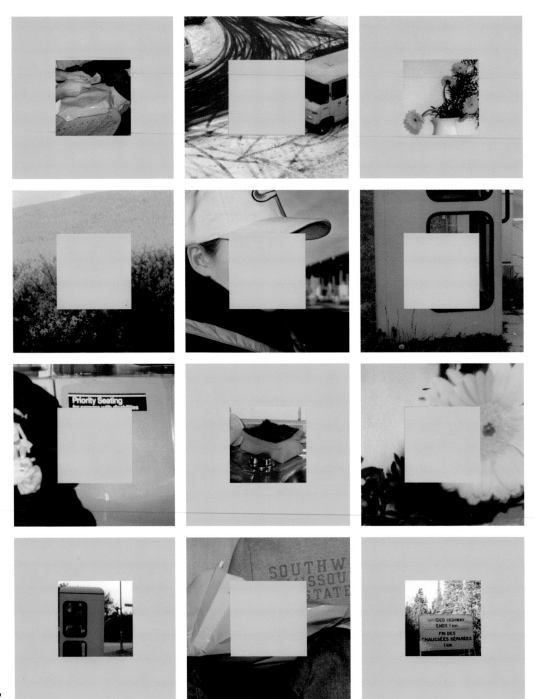

The collection and ordering of seemingly unrelated imagery.
A formal connection is created through colour or a pattern. The
content can relate a story.

By collecting and arranging pictures of the same theme, subject matter can be bundled and hence become more concentrated and insistent.

IMAGE CONTRASTS

coloured – black and white

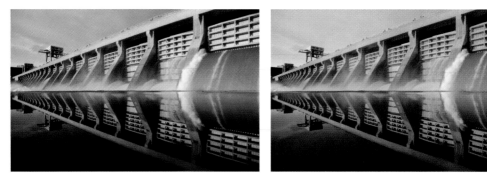

concrete – abstract

in focus – out of focus

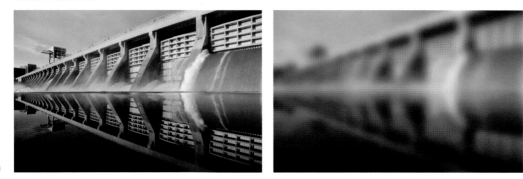

technological – natural

the whole – a detail

clear – opaque

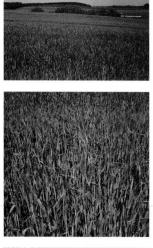

By duplication of a striking image or image structure and by displacing, rotating, flipping or distorting the copies, new forms or structures with ornamental character can be created.

IMAGE ORGANISATION

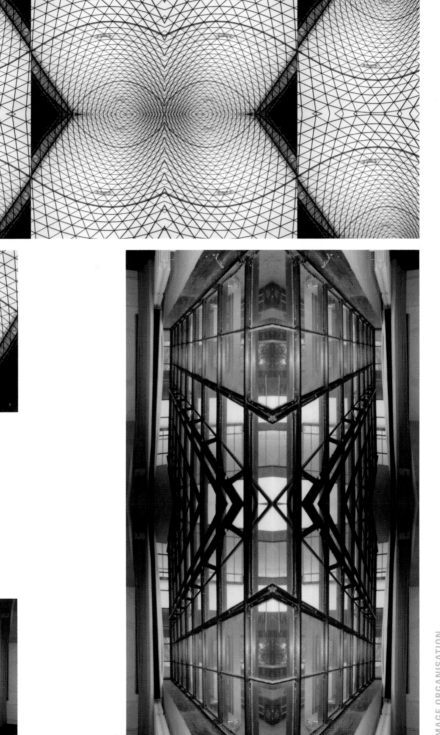

Transparency can suggest or support spatial impressions. Something that is less transparent seems further away. By combining transparent and non-transparent image areas, spatial staggering can be achieved.

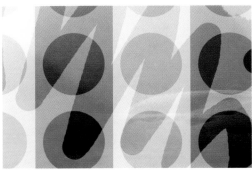

In Photoshop, transparency is a design tool easily applied, for instance by changing the opacity of layers. Additionally, the opacity settings for different layers and actions like "Duplicate layer..." and "Merge" from the "Layer menu options" can be combined. Create a white layer to cover an image in Photoshop. Experiment with the opacity settings for the white layer. On new white layers punch out geometrical shapes of differing number, size and arrangement (select a shape and delete selection).

IMAGE ORGANISATION

247

IMAGE PROCESSES

Image processes can be achieved by manipulating the image and positioning and re-positioning it in a layout grid. Prior to this they can consciously be designed on the shoot. The results can be series that contain a temporal dimension, e.g. motion sequences in nature or technology (running tap water, blazing fire, cloud forming, building site) or motion sequences of the body, in which each state is photographically recorded.

Of course it is also possible to manipulate a process of nature. The image on the left was composed by arranging shells and pebbles in a temporally and spatially limited shadow cast. The white pebbles are positioned in the shade, the dark pebbles in the area exposed to the sun. Weather and time of day were part of the planning process for this image process. The sequence on the right shows the effect of surf, that washes over the sand with irregular intervals, progressively washing away footprints, or in this case letters that had been finger-written in the sand, until we are eventually left again with a smooth beach. It pays off to study these unstable conditions of the environment closely and to integrate them in the planning of the image.

Manipulation of colour. Which one is the original? (Manipulation in Photoshop using "Image → Adjust → Replace Colour…".)

Manipulation of parts of the image can change the image information drastically. (Manipulation in Photoshop using "Edit → Paste Into" to paste parts of the image or of a different image into a selection.)

IMAGE ORGANISATION

Manipulation of image parts can put image information into a new context. (Complex manipulation and retouching in Photoshop through image montage with "layer masks" and various "layer modes".)

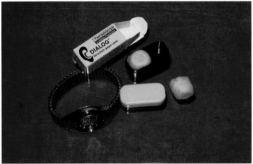

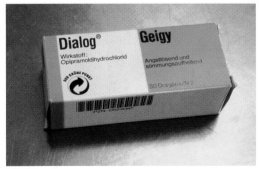

Image montages can visualise artistic ideas, as shown in this case.

Via Lewandowsky, design for the competition "Art In The Public Space", Bremen, 2002. (Printed by kind permission of the artist.)

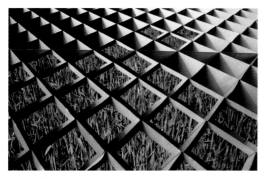

Image manipulation
can simulate the
illusion of absurd
realities.

QUOTATIONS AND RECOMMENDED READING

(Books marked ■ are suitable additional reading to widen and deepen your knowledge on the computer applications discussed in this book.)

■ Binder, Martin. "A Typographical Handbook". Würzburg: DiploMartin, 1995

■ Bittl, Klaus Rudolf. "Photoshop for the Web. Design visual Websites". Reinbek: Rowohlt Taschenbuch Publishing, 2001

■ Brody, Neville. "The Graphic Language of Neville Brody". New York: Rizzoli, 1988

■ Bühler, Peter. "The Medium Colour. analogue and digital". Itzehoe: Publisher Beruf und Schule, 1998

■ Carson, David. "David Carson 2: The End of Print". Schopfheim: Bangert Publishing, 1997

■ Donner, Harald, and Hans-Christian Kuhnow and Andreas Pankalla. "Freehand: know how. Effective Design for Print and Web. For Mac and PC". Reinbek: Rowohlt Taschenbuch Publishing, 2000

■ Douté, Kathrin. "QuarkXPress 4. Solutions for Users. For Mac and PC". Reinbek: Rowohlt Taschenbuch Publishing, 1998

■ Ernst, Bruno, Hg. "The Magic Mirror of M.C. Escher". Berlin. Taco Publishing and Agency, 1986

■ Fossmann, Friedrich, and Hans Peter Willberg. "Typography For Reading". Mayence Publishing Hermann Schmidt, 1997

■ Friedl, Friedrich, and Nicolaus Ott and Bernhard Stein. "when who how". Cologne: Könemann, 1998

■ Frutiger, Adrian. "Man And His Symbols. Typefaces, Symbols, Logos, Signals". Paris; Dreieich: Weiss Publishing; Wiesbaden: Imprint for Fourier Publishing, 1991

■ Gansweid, Jürgen. "Symmetry and Design. Optical Motion Effects Developed With Geometrical Elements". Munich: Callwey, 1987

■ Gekeler, Hans. "Handbook On Colour. Systematic, Aesthetic, Practical". Cologne: DuMont, 2000

■ Gerritsen, F. "Development of Colour Theory". Göttingen: 1984

■ Heller, Eva. "How Colour Works".

Hamburg, 1989

■ Holzschlag, Molly E. "Colour For Websites". Reinbek: Rowohlt Taschenbuch Publishing, 2002

■ Jenny, Peter. "Image Concepts. The Well-Ordered Chaos". Mayence: Publishing H. Schmidt, 2000

■ Jenny, Peter. "Notes on Drawing Technique". Mayence: Publishing H. Schmidt, 1999

■ Kandinsky, W. "Dot And Line On The Surface". Bern: Benteli Publishing, 1973

■ Kapitzki, Herbert. "Programmed Design". Karlsruhe: 1980

■ Khazaeli, Cyrus Dominik. "Crash Course Typo And Layout. From Design Of Typefaces To The Visual Concept". Reinbek: Rowohlt Taschenbuch Publishing, 2001

■ Küthe, Erich, and Susanne Küthe. "Marketing With Patterns". Cologne: DuMont, 1998

■ Küthe, Erich, and Matteo Thun. "Marketing With Images. Management with Trend Tables, Mood Charts, Storyboards, Photographic montages, Collages". Cologne: DuMont, 1995

■ Küthe, Erich, and Axel Venn. "Marketing With Colours". Cologne: DuMont, 1996

■ Leary, Michael. "Web Designer's Guide to Typography". Hayden Books

■ Leu, Olaf, and Frieder Mellinghoff, Type Directors Club of New York, Hg. "Word Image Word. Producing A Message". Mayence: Publishing Hermann Schmidt, 1989

■ Lewandowsky, Pina. "Photoshop 6. Solutions For Users. For Mac and PC". Reinbek: Rowohlt Taschenbuch Publishing, 2001

■ Lewandowsky, Pina. "Photoshop: Know How. Effective Design For Print And Web. For Mac and PC". Reinbek: Rowohlt Taschenbuch Publishing, 2000

■ Luidl, Philipp. "Typography. Basic Knowledge". Deutscher Drucker, 1996

■ Matthaei, Jörg Michael. "Basic Questions of Graphic Design. Perceiving And Designing". Augsburg: Augustus Publishing, 1990 (currently out of print)

■ Maurer, Fritz. "Colour Reproduction. Training Material For Electronic Image Reproduction". Buchs, Switzerland: A&F Maurer, Publishing, 1995

■ McKelvey, Roy. "Hypergraphics. Design And Architecture Of Websites". Reinbek: Rowohlt Taschenbuch

Publishing, 1999

■ Müller-Brockmann, Josef. "Grid Systems For Visual Design". Teufen, Switzerland: Niggli Publishing, 1996

■ Müller, Monika, and Hans Peter Willberg. "Type Recognition. A Typology Of Typefaces For Graphic Designers, Type Setters, Book Dealers And Art Teachers". Ravensburg: Otto Maier Publishing, 1981

■ Nikkels, Walter. "The Space Of The Book". Cologne: Tropen Publishing, 1998

■ Ott, Ernst. "Optimal Reading". Deutscher Buecher Bund

■ Pankalla, Andreas. "Freehand. Version 9 and 10. For Mac And PC". Reinbek: Rowohlt Taschenbuch Publishing, 2002

■ Pankalla, Andreas, and Harald Donner. "Illustrator 10. Solutions For Users. For Mac and PC". Reinbek: Rowohlt Taschenbuch Publishing, 2002

■ Siegle, Michael Bernd. "Logo. Basics Of Visual Sign Design. An Introduction to Graphic Design Using Logo Design". Itzehoe: Beruf und Schule Publishing, 1996

■ Spiekermann, Erik. "Cause & Effect. A Typographical Novel". Erlangen: Context Publishing, 1982

■ Stankowski, Anton, and Karl Duschek. "Visual Communication. Design Handbook". Berlin: Dietrich Reimer Publishing, 1994

■ Tschichold, Jan. "Typefaces 1925–1975, Bd. 1 and 2". Brinkmann & Bose

■ Turtschi, Ralf. "Practical Typography". Teufen, Switzerland: Niggli Publishing, 2000

■ Williams, Robert. "The Mac (PC) Is Not A Typewriter". Zurich: Midas Publishing, 1993

■ Württembergischer Kunstverein, Hg. "Bauhaus Graphics. 50 Years Of Bauhaus". Stuttgart: Sonderkatalog, Württembergischer Kunstverein, 1968

■ Ziegler, Ulf Erdmann, and Nicolaus Ott and Bernhard Stein. "From Word To Image And Back". Berlin: Ernst and Sohn, Publishing For Architecture And Technical Sciences, 1992

■ Zuffo, Dario. "Basics Of Visual Design". Liechtenstein, Switzerland: Niggli Publishing, 1998

INDEX

Aligning 26, Text 210, 211
Animation 18, 54, 55, 56, 90
Appearance, Sensation 10, 17, 70, 126, 138, 163, 176
Attach to path (text) (Freehand) 32, 33, 212
Attributes 17, 126
Baseline Grid (QuarkXPress) 208
Basic elements 14, 58, 187
Basic shapes 79, 172, 173, 187, 190
Blur 109, 130
Body colours (CMYK) 136
Brightness / tonal value 100, 152, 186
Centre of gravity development 62–65, 85
Cloning (Freehand) 40, 90, 91
Coincidence 23, 27
Collecting and ordering, Images 220
Colour contrasts 158, 168, 172, 177, 182
Colour definition, CMYK-colours 136, (Freehand) 150, (QuarkXPress) 151
Colour gradation/colour wedge 152
Colour impression 139
Colour impression 158, 168
Colour physiology/psychology 138
Colour saturation 152, 176
Colour selection (Photoshop) 168, 182
Colour star/colour circle 148
Colour tones 87, 89, 168
Colours: Primary, Secondary, Tertiary 149, 186
Combinatorics principle 40–44, 73
Combine (Freehand) 18
Complementary colours 156
Composition 63, 64, 68–72, 77, 78, 82, 84, 87, 88, 164
Contour 36, 96
Contrast 75, 78, 79, 100, 175, 176, 240, 241
Convert to paths (text) 36
Covering 192, 214, 215
Cross hatching 123
Cut, Paste Inside (Freehand) 18, 27, 71, 80, 81, 87
Cut out (Photoshop) 83, 89, 132
Cutting tool (Freehand) 40
Density 38, 72, 88, 102
Detail 11, 18, 21, 27, 36, 37, 79, 222
Direction 25, 28, 39, 190
Displacing (horizontal, vertical) 34
Distance 26, 100, 205,
Division (Freehand) 81, 195, 200
Dot 8, 12, 18, 123
Drawing 46–59, 90, 127
Dynamic 35, 39, 75
Figure-floor relation 37, 68, 72, 77, 79, 95, 102, 132, 172

Filter (Photoshop) 130
Folder principle 40, 42, 43, 73
Format 11, 62, 66, 71, 75–78, 86, 87, 204
Grade (DTP programs) 105, 118,191
Grey effect, (Text) 30, 78, 86 104, 124
Grey tone 108
Grid 38, 122, 188, 204, 209
Grid definition (programs) 16, 20, 40, 194
Guides definition (Freehand) 20, 194
Harmony 71, 110, 180
Image manipulation 250–253
Image organisation 220
Image processes 248, 249
Image, Scan 198, 220
Inner form 36, 37, 76, 80, 174,
Kerning (letter spacing) 31, 35
Kerning 104
Layer (Photoshop) 20
Layer mode (Photoshop) 180, 181
Layout 64, 65, 85, 188, 204
Layout sketch, scribble 65, 85, 204, 207
Leading 30, 35, 104
Legibility 104, 174, 175
Light colours 136
Light-dark/light and shade 90, 116
Line 22–37, 120
Line thickness/stroke 26, 100
Line types 25
Mask (Photoshop) 20, 82, 83
Master page (QuarkXPress) 205
Media 186
Mix (Freehand) 110, 153, 157
Modulations rows 110, 154, 182
Motif-plane analysis 89, 132
Motion 28, 29, 39
Negative (inversion) 156
Opacity (Photoshop) 58, 127, 180
Optical Phenomena 24, 30, 75, 117, 121, 176, 177
Order 31, 43, 220
Ornament 41, 43, 44, 73, 90, 91
Overlay 102, 114, 178
Overprint (Freehand/QuarkXPress) 178
Page proportions 66
Passe-partout (Freehand) 18, 21, 62,
Passe-partout 11, 18, 20, 21, 62, 71, 110
Path operations (Freehand) 81
Path tool (Photoshop) 20
Pattern 41, 73, 90, 91
Perception, rules 92–97
Permutation 40, 42
Perspective 102, 114, 170, 242, 243
Pixelate (Mosaic filter/ Photoshop) 109, 155
Plan, Orientation 57, 58, 59

Plane 18, 60, 77
Plane Division 62, 64, 77, 212
Position 13, 14, 24, 25, 28, 69–72
Positioning 13, 17, 20, 21, 24, 25, 28, 32, 60, 76, 77, 84, 103, 212
Print area 205
Progression 18, 19, 24, 26, 35, 100
Progressive growing (Freehand) 18, 19, 24, 26, 35
Proportion 19, 21, 22, 23, 36, 68, 84, 86, 88, 166, 196, 200, 212
Punch (Freehand) 18, 195
Quantity 15, 166, 168
Rapport 44
Repetition 16, 26, 34, 40, 41, 42, 43, 44, 71, 73, 75, 90, 91
Rhythm 31, 35, 41, 105
Rows 38
Seeing, to learn 49
Shape arrangement 37, 70, 71, 212
Shape contrasts 74, 172, 173
Shape deconstruction 90, 190
Shape impression 39, 138, 163, 170, 177, 178, 212
Shape relation, Overview 75
Signs, logo, icons 89, 173, 190
Size 14, 174
Sketch (Scribble) 49
Spatial experience 39
Spatiality 102, 114, 170, 171
Step and Repeat (Quark Xpress) 18, 26, 34, 71 88, 90, 164
Structure 38, 100, 121, 186, 188
Super characters 42
Symmetry 38, 210, 211, 245
Tabs 33
Tension (Vibrancy) 21, 36, 39, 68, 72, 76, 77, 78, 82, 86, 88, 196, 200, 212
Text as strip 84, 87
Texture 100, 124, 186
Tiling (Freehand) 44
Tone separation 122
Tracing (Photoshop) 58, 127
Transform (Freehand) 42, 71, 87, 121, 131, (Photoshop) 244, 245
Transparency 178, 246, 247
Type size 107
Type style 104
Typefaces 80
Typography 35, 36, 76, 104, 197, 210
Visualising expressions 77, 78, 84, 87, 145, 163, 175
Volumes 114
Word spacing 31, 35, 105

PHOTOGRAPHIC CREDITS

Representational photographs of art that
are not mentioned here have been made
available from the artists' archives by their
generous permission.

- Borchert, Jan: pp. 251
- Davies, Bevan: pp. 99 (Anderson)
- Lewandowsky, Pina: pp. 122, 236, 237, 239,
  241, 242, 243, 246, 247; © Image
  manipulation & image montage
  pp. 245, 250, 253
- Lewandowsky, Via: pp. 251 (image
  retouching Jan Borchert), pp. 252
- Morell, Wolfgang: pp. 184 (Sigmar Polke)
- Neuhaus, David: "Skater" pp. 224
- PhotoDisc/Getty Images (by kind
  permission): pp. 125, 126, 127, 143, 240,
  241, 253
- Schönborn, Philipp (by kind permission):
  pp. 135 (Geiger)
- Zeischegg, Francis: pp. 222–225, 230–235,
  238, 244, 245, 248, 249, 250;
  image montage pp. 133
- Zeischegg, Irmgard: pp. 213, 215, 217,
  226, 229